Flight Plan

The Travel Hacker's Guide to Free World
Travel & Getting Paid on the Road

By: Zephan Moses Blaxberg

Printed in the United States of America

Year of Purpose Publishing, 2018
Paperback ISBN-13: 978-0-9969599-5-7
Kindle ISBN-13: 978-0-9969599-6-4

Book cover designed courtesy of Fiverr Seller Armejndi, Armend Meha, http://www.zephanmoses.com/armend
Editing by Wayne H. Purdin
http://www.zephanmoses.com/waynehpurdin

Legal Disclaimer:

Although the author and publisher have made every effort to ensure that the information in this book was correct at press time, the author and publisher don't assume, and hereby disclaim, any liability to any party for any loss, damage, or disruption caused by errors or omissions, whether such errors or omissions result from negligence, accident, or any other cause.

This book isn't intended as a substitute for the legal advice of lawyers or financial advice from a financial planner or accountant. The reader should regularly consult a financial planner, accountant, and lawyer in matters relating to his/her actions and particularly with respect to any decisions that may require consultation or legal opinion.

The information in this book is meant to supplement your travel & financial knowledge. Like any activity involving travel, spending money, applying for credit cards, and making money online, this activity poses some inherent risk. The authors and publisher advise readers to take full responsibility for their safety and know their limits. Before practicing the skills described in this book, be sure that your credit score is well maintained, and don't take risks beyond your level of experience, aptitude, financial standing, and comfort level.

With that said, travel hacking can be fun and rewarding and ultimately boost your credit score. Many people have created careers or part-time hobbies out of doing it (myself included). If a financial, travel, or employment decision doesn't feel right, don't do it. Let your intuition be your guide and enjoy the ride.

Affiliate Disclaimer:

I've always been a huge proponent of transparency; thus, I'm disclosing to you that I've included certain products, services, and apps in this book that I may earn an affiliate commission for in any purchases that you make. My goal is to help educate you on the possibilities for making money. You should assume that any links leading you to a product or service could be an affiliate link where I receive compensation just to be safe. With that said, I do my best to only promote products or services that I've experimented with. If you have any questions regarding the above, please don't hesitate to contact me!

Table of Contents

Dedication

To my beautiful fiancé, Mollye, winner of my heart and my companion pass. I can't wait to see the world with you.

Introduction

As I logged into my Southwest Airlines account, I sat back for a second and let out a sigh of relief. In just a matter of weeks, my rewards points balance had increased from around 3,000 (which gets you nothing) to over 125,000 points.

According to Nerdwallet.com, 125,000 Rapid Rewards Points with Southwest Airlines are worth approximately $1,200-1,400 in free travel (https://www.nerdwallet.com/blog/reward-program-reviews/southwest-rapid-rewards-points/). All I had to do was take out a credit card and spend some money on it (you'll learn how to do this later).

This was the mother lode of all travel hacks, as it pushed me over the tipping point of earning half a million total skymiles/rewards points in less than three years.

As an added bonus, I also received notice that I'd be getting a free companion pass for the next eighteen months. This means a companion of my choosing gets to fly with me absolutely free wherever I go. We simply pay the government taxes and fees, which, in the case of Southwest Airlines, is a mere $5.60 per flight.

Having this companion pass effectively doubled the value of my 125K points to just under $3,000 worth of free travel.

Travel hacking leverages credit cards, so I pulled out my phone and discovered my credit score had only taken a hit of 4 points, dropping it down to a laughable 820. For reference, the highest credit score you can possibly get is 850 (which is a good thing and nearly unattainable). I'll share more about this later as well.

It's funny looking back at the time when I would pay hundreds of dollars to fly because I had no idea what I was about to embark upon when I first heard the words *travel hacking.*

After three years of free travel, seeing 35 out of 50 states within the U.S. and getting paid to visit Italy, Slovenia, Vatican City, England, France, Netherlands, and Belgium, I decided it was time to share with the world how it can be done. I've also been able to visit Jamaica, Haiti, and Mexico on the cheap and plan to do a trip to Southeast Asia in the very near future.

As I write this, I'm currently booking trips to North Carolina, Las Vegas, and Wisconsin for later this month, all for free. For some of them, I'm actually getting paid!

Can you imagine what it would be like to travel the United States or even the world and get paid to do it? My new "normal" is traveling one to five times per month.

Throughout this book, you're going to find lessons and advice in three main categories:

1. Travel Hacking
2. Financial Responsibility
3. Digital Nomad Employment

I mentioned it in the disclaimer but I have to say this again: travel hacking isn't for everyone. Leaving a box of donuts on the counter in your office isn't the best way to make everyone happy. Some people love donuts; others, who are watching their diet, might not want to partake, and that's okay! But you have to have the proper self-control to know when the donut is worth eating and when you should pass.

Some readers of this book will take the tools shared here to the umpteenth degree. For example, I took out 15 credit cards in my first three years of travel hacking. If you have a low credit score or you've experienced bankruptcy, divorce, collections, or a combination of all three, you'll be starting from a different point. You'll mostly focus on building good credit so that in the future you can travel for free.

Regardless of whether you're a world traveler or not, all I ask is that you take into consideration that this book is here to teach you valuable financial lessons, ways to make money online, and, most importantly, help you overcome the fear & uncertainty of living your dream life on the road.

In this book, I'm going to teach the exact tools and strategies I deployed to obtain free world travel. Like any loophole or workaround, the strategies are constantly changing, so it's crucial that you pay attention to the blogs and articles mentioned here. I also urge you to do more of your own research once you understand the strategies at play. Many of the techniques I used when I first started this hobby are not available anymore, so I'm only going to teach actionable systems that still work at the time of writing this book.

On another note, travel hacking does involve making financial decisions. There will be times when I recommend credit cards and discuss credit scores, and I realize that everyone is in a different place financially. Thus, please make wise decisions based on the information I've provided here. No one wants to go into debt just to travel the world, and no one should have to. I'll be teaching you how to improve your credit score if it isn't good enough, and I'll explain to the best of my abilities how to keep a good credit score.

If you feel unsure after reading anything here, please reach out to an expert, whether that be an accountant, financial advisor, lawyer, or other professional.

Travel hacking takes patience and effort; just know that your starting point may be different than someone else's. It takes time to reap the rewards, but the rewards are very generous. My results are certainly in a top percentile, and it's a great feeling when you reach the top. I believe that if you apply yourself to the skills and principles laid out in this book, you too will find yourself in this elite group of free world travelers.

Welcome to *Flight Plan.*

Chapter 1: What Is Travel Hacking?

Travel hacking, by my definition, is simply a methodology that frequent travelers leverage so that they can continue traveling for free or at discounted rates.

At its core and for the sake of this book, I'm going to define travel hacking as taking advantage of credit card signup and bonus offers so that you can obtain skymiles and rewards points. Oftentimes, this will be free or at little cost to you.

Travel hacking involves five steps that will be discussed in depth later. Here are the five steps you need to know to get up and moving (literally):

1. Build Good Credit
2. Take Out a Travel Rewards Credit Card
3. Hit the Spending Bonus
4. Pay Off the Credit Card
5. Redeem Rewards for Free (or discounted) Travel

It's important to mention that, currently, travel hacking in this form is really only available to citizens in the United States and countries that offer credit card signup bonuses.

Building Good Credit

Credit cards can be your friend, but they can also be your enemy. I've seen many people refuse to take out credit cards due to their lack of self-control, and I know people who have far too many cards because they can't afford their bills.

Regardless of your status, credit runs the world around these parts. If you want to buy a house, you need credit. Are you looking to lease a car? Credit. Credit is what allows banks to determine if you're a good candidate for borrowing their money. They take into consideration many factors and ultimately decide if you're worthy of a loan.

We'll dive deeper into credit, but, for now, just know that there are many financial aspects of credit, and your credit score must be in good standing before you start to hack.

Take Out a Travel Rewards Credit Card

Credit card companies in the United States (and a few other countries) love to rope people in with bonuses. For some cards, you may receive bonus points that can be redeemed for gift cards or cash back. In many instances, a credit card will give you special discounts in retail stores or simply the flexibility to pay off bills with little to no interest.

Specific credit cards are ideal when it comes to redeeming travel rewards. The offers are always changing, but some of the best deals will go something like this...

"Limited-time offer! Earn 60,000 points when you spend $2,000 on purchases in the first three months. $69 annual fee applied on your first statement. Apply now."

This particular offer came from a Southwest Airlines Chase credit card that rewards you with 60K Southwest Rapid Rewards points once you've spent two grand in the first three months.

If that amount seems daunting, don't worry about it just yet. We'll discuss a strategy called "Manufactured Spending" that can take care of hitting the spending limit.

If you'd like to start by looking at credit card options, a brief Google search for your *favorite airline name* + "credit card" will do the trick. But please don't apply for anything until after you've finished reading this book!

Hit the Spending Bonus

As I previously mentioned, the trick to gaining a large sum of skymiles or rewards points is to spend a certain amount of money on a credit card within the promotional timeline they mention. For the specific card mentioned above, it was three months. Every card will be different but the most common period is ninety days.

For many people, there are ways to spend $2,000 in less than three months or even one month. But I realize that this isn't the case for your average Joe or Jane. I don't want to reveal too much about this just yet, so continue reading and we'll come back to this part later.

Pay Off the Credit Card

As with any credit card, you're taking a line of credit from a bank. At the end of the day, when you spend money by swiping that piece of plastic, you're making a pact with a company that you'll pay back the amount of money you've borrowed monthly. If you don't pay back the money that was borrowed, you'll be subject to fines, penalties, and interest.

The one lesson you must learn is to pay off your credit card bills each month.

For some, this is common sense, but for others, this is news. For each month that you're not paying off your credit card debt, you typically will incur interest. Sometimes, interest can be as high as 19-25%, which is astronomical.

Let's suppose, for example, you have a credit card with an interest rate of 17% APR. If you were to charge $1,000 in purchases onto the credit card and you only pay a minimum payment of $100 each month, you'll rack up over $86 in interest charges, and it's going to take you eleven months to pay it off. That's $86 that you didn't have to pay the bank if you had managed your money, only buy what you can afford and pay off your bill each month.

Some people have financial struggles, and I understand that this happens from time to time. People fall into bad luck, lose their job, make poor choices, etc. The list goes on and on, but there are ways to get out of debt, and if you don't have any debt, just be sure not to get *into* debt.

Redeem Rewards for Free

Every credit card that provides rewards points for your spending habits will also have a rewards portal online. Usually, you'll log in to pay your credit card bill, and there will be a place to redeem your points. In the case of most of your big-name airlines, your points typically transfer into your skymiles or rewards account without the need to go through your credit card company. For some cards that aren't tied to any particular airline, however, you'll go through their system for booking.

These are the basics behind travel hacking. In my eyes, it's one of the simplest ways to accrue rewards points and travel the world. There are many other ways to do this, but for the sake of keeping up with the curve and not providing you with an outdated method, this is one that has remained the same since I started taking out credit cards over a decade ago.

Now, let's move into discussing who travel hacking is for.

Chapter 2: Who Is Travel Hacking For?

Travel hacking requires a few different skills and personality traits, some of which may be new to you. Travel hacking is ideal for someone who has schedule flexibility, a good sense of their financials, and excellent organizational skills, and it can't hurt to have the ability to spend money.

In fact, if you make large purchases, you'll find it much easier to make this happen in a short time. In less than thirty days (assuming you can pay off your bills), you could easily obtain your first free round-trip flight.

Schedule Flexibility

When traveling, some of the best (read cheapest) flights leave at 5am and arrive home around midnight or 1 a.m. You could save thousands of rewards points by taking the inconvenient flights that most others don't want to take.

This is one of the best ways to keep your precious points for the times when you really need or want to travel.

Deals pop up much of the time when you can only fly within certain dates. Some of my friends have traveled to Australia, Iceland, Italy, and more because they found a flight deal and were able to get off from work.

If you work for a company that has flexible vacation time or if you work remotely, you'll be an ideal candidate for last-minute deals.

This doesn't mean that you can't travel hack just because you aren't flexible. But it's a good reminder of how job flexibility can expand your ability to see the world. That's why we built a whole section into this book all about how to make money on the road.

One thing to note is that not all flights that leave at inconvenient times are cheap. You may want to look at surrounding airports. For example, if I live in Baltimore, Maryland, my home base is Baltimore Washington International (BWI) Airport. But a 35-mile drive away is Dulles Airport in Washington DC. Dulles is a much larger airport, and, on many occasions, can be cheaper because of the number of flights going in and out.

You could also take a $15 bus ride from Baltimore to New York and fly out of JFK, LaGuardia, or Newark Airports. Flexibility is key with your timing but also with your departure and return locations. Keep this in mind for future reference.

A Good Sense of Financials

If you're the type of person who checks their bank statements or credit card statements to make sure there are no odd charges, you're going to fit right in here. When it comes to hitting credit card bonuses, you want to be able to keep track of how much money you've spent on each card. You also want to guarantee that you won't miss a statement; otherwise, you can be hit with late payment penalties.

I'm also going to ask you to follow instructions later to discover what your credit score is, and, depending on where you fall on the ladder, you may need to complete certain exercises to increase your score.

You don't have to be great at math, but travel hacking does involve paying attention to numbers and fine print.

Excellent Organizational Skills

It should be fairly obvious by now that managing multiple credit cards, payments, and rewards accounts takes some organization. You'll want to make calendar reminders to check your bills and statements. You may even want to keep a written record of everything because some credit card companies have limits and rules surrounding how many cards you can take out and how long you need to wait before getting another card.

I can't stress enough how travel hacking isn't a simple arcade machine. You can't just place a quarter in the slot, move a claw around, and get a prize in less than thirty seconds. Could you realistically get a free flight by this time next month? Absolutely, but just like an arcade machine, it has to be under the right circumstances. Not everyone hits the jackpot on the first try.

Chapter 3: Who Is Travel Hacking Not For?

A lot of people would reach this point and think that, since they have poor credit, travel hacking isn't for them. However, this is completely wrong. Travel hacking should be the goal you place on a pedestal because it will encourage you to manage your money better. It's the big reward for paying off bills, working your way out of debt, and getting to a secure financial situation.

Remember, credit isn't just required for travel hacking. Having a good credit score will benefit you when you need to buy/lease your next car, for buying a house, and, sometimes, to even rent an apartment.

So, let's look at who travel hacking isn't for:

- The corporate employee who never gets a day off
- The entrepreneur who hasn't gotten their business off the ground yet

- The stay-at-home mom who's paying off student loan debt from ten years ago
- The person who's always looking to make a quick buck without putting in the work
- The divorcee who had their credit ruined
- The person who just declared an $80,000 bankruptcy

Could travel hacking be a good thing for these people eventually? Absolutely. But it's important to know when you don't have the foundational skills required to put in the effort and clean up your credit.

I don't want to sound mean and certainly hope this doesn't come off as impossible. Just know that there are important pieces of this book that will be catered more to you than someone who has an impeccable credit score.

Time is one of the biggest solutions for anyone who might have a similar situation to those listed above. But the biggest solution of all is knowledge and a willingness to put in the work.

I have people call me weekly, saying, "I want to go to Florida in three weeks; how can I do it for free?"

The answer is you can't, unless you've put in the months of work needed to rack up rewards points. Travel hacking isn't for you if you're shortsighted and don't think about the long-term impact of your actions.

But enough about all the reasons why you can't travel hack. Let's move on to talking about what travel hacking did for me and can do for you too.

Chapter 4: What It Can Lead To

In May of 2013, I left my full-time job working at the Apple Store. I couldn't take it anymore, working in a retail position. It takes a certain type of person to work in a customer service role under a large corporation.

Often, it can feel like you're a small blade of grass in a field of rolling hills. I know that I felt constrained and wanted greater freedom in my time as well as life.

A few short months later, I was on a weekend retreat where I hiked up the side of a cliff. I was thinking about what it meant to me to be able to take four days off from my business. I thought about how amazing it would feel to be able to travel every month without worrying about my financial situation or any other issues that were bothering me at the time.

At that time, I knew I wanted to travel more. In fact, I wanted to travel almost every month. I saw it as a way to recharge and meet new people. I could experience new foods, cultures, and customs. I felt that traveling allowed me to peel away the layers of the onion that's Zephan and see what person I could become when I removed the security of always having a car and being able to just go. I realized that travel would increase my bubble of awareness.

Every person will have their own reasons for travel, but my life has been quite enjoyable since making the leap.

I now own my own business. I choose the people I want to work with, when I want to work with them, and how I'll work with them. I can schedule a vacation or business trip each month because I now have the ability to do so without worrying about the cost of the flight. If I want to take a day trip from my hometown in Baltimore, Maryland up to Portland, Maine to get a lobster sandwich and still make it home in time for my favorite TV shows, I can.

There are many benefits to owning a business, but if you structure your schedule for flexibility, travel hacking can completely change your life.

I've also been fortunate enough to produce a popular podcast called "The Year of Purpose Podcast," (www.zephanmoses.com) where I had the chance to interview over 200 entrepreneurs from all over the world who created life on their own terms. This podcast surpassed 120,000 downloads in just over two years and led to the chance of a lifetime to give a TEDx talk at my alma mater, James Madison University. To view the TEDx talk, visit http://www.zephanmoses.com/tedx.

Around the same time, I published my first book, *Life Re-Scripted: Find Your Purpose and Design Your Dream Life*

Before the Curtains Close and my three adult mandala coloring and gratitude journals, *Greatfull*.

Twenty-year-old me leaving college could never predict that my life would be this way in seven years but hindsight is twenty-twenty.

If you're hesitant to start travel hacking or even just to embark on your dream adventure, please don't let fear stop you from moving forward. You have such little time on this earth, and, as Brendon Burchard said, "At the end of our lives, we all ask, 'Did I live? Did I love? Did I matter?'" You can't afford to not see everything the world has to offer.

Chapter 5: Credit Score 101

How is travel hacking related to a credit score?

Travel hacking is defined differently for everyone. For some, it's paying close attention to airline prices and buying a "mistake" fare. For others, it's leveraging credit card signup bonuses to rack up skymiles points.

I'll mention some tools to land the best airfare deals later on, but for the next few chapters on leveraging credit cards, we'll be looking at travel hacking from the latter, using special promotions and offers combined with spending tactics to hit bonus spends within a short time.

This is where your credit score comes in.

Any time you're dealing with something financially related, whether it's a credit card, car lease, or buying (or renting) a house, you're impacting your credit score.

We'll talk more about what a credit score is in the next section, but just know that as long as you're using the strategies to gain points with a credit card, it will have an effect on your score.

What is a credit score?

So what is a credit score? It's something that most people don't pay attention to until after college, and it only really becomes a concern when you've entered "the real world."

In nontechnical terms, a credit score is a three-digit number that represents how creditworthy you are. It's based on a number of financial stats and allows a company to tell if you're a safe bet when it comes to lending money.

Lenders such as banks and credit card companies use this score to determine if they're taking a high risk in providing you with money you don't already have.

You may also find that companies like your Internet provider or cell-phone service provider will check your credit score because they want to make sure that you'll pay your bills on time and in full.

In the United States (where most travel hacking is easily done), there are three major credit reporting bureaus: Experian, TransUnion, and Equifax. There are different methods to calculating your score, and each of these companies manage it a little bit differently.

In the end, companies only really look at one or two of these reporting bureaus to make their decision.

You can also get your credit report completely free once every twelve months by visiting annualcreditreport.com, but be cautious about any other site that promises to do the same for a fee. You'll be able to leverage the Credit Karma app to see your score, but the report is the only way to view past and existing credit agreements. This includes credit cards, mortgages, car loans, student loans, and inquiries into your score. More to come on this later.

What impacts your credit score?

Your credit score will go up or down regularly. Think of it like the stock market being altered by supply and demand.

Don't worry if one week, your score drops by ten points because the next week, it will magically climb by twenty points. You should become concerned only if the numbers change drastically.

The following six factors affect your credit score:

- Credit Card Use
- Payment History
- Derogatory Marks
- Credit Age
- Total Accounts
- Hard Inquiries

Credit card use is how much credit you're using compared to your total limit. So, if you have two credit cards and each of them has a line of credit of $5,000, then you have a total limit of $10,000. If you're balance is $500, then you're only utilizing 5% of your overall credit.

Credit card companies like to see that you aren't maxing out your cards. It makes you less of a liability and more of an asset when you pay down your credit card bills.

Credit use has a high impact on your score, so you want to keep your balances low and check in regularly to make sure you aren't using a high percentage.

As long as you stay below roughly 30% of your total credit card limit, you'll stay in the green with a fantastic credit score.

Payment history is another important aspect of your credit score. It has a high impact on your number, and it's plain and simple – have you made all of your payments on time?

If you check your credit report and find that you've had late payments in the past, it may be worth calling your company to tell them you made a mistake and to ask if they would be able to take it off your report. Be sure to offer to pay down any existing balance on the card while you're on the phone.

Derogatory marks are another high-impact factor. This includes things like collections, tax liens, bankruptcies, or civil judgments. These marks can stay on your report for seven to ten years, so it's crucial to make sure you don't get any in the first place.

If you ever have bills that go to collections, take care of them right away!

Having zero derogatory marks keeps you in the green, but once you have one or two, you very quickly move into the yellow zone.

Next up is credit age or how long you've had your credit cards. This is an average number of how many years you've had credit, so if you took your first and only credit card out five years ago, your average age is five years. However, if you took out one card five years ago and another card out yesterday, your average age will be two and a half years.

Lenders usually want to see that you have experience in using credit responsibly over a long time, so just keep in mind that the sooner you open a credit card and leave it open, the better. You don't want to close old cards, as that will reduce your credit age.

We'll talk more about closing cards later, but the rule of thumb is, if it doesn't cost you anything to keep it open, don't remove the card.

The last two pieces of your credit score are total number of accounts and hard inquiries.

Believe it or not, having more accounts is better. I know this sounds counterintuitive, but they base your total accounts on your total number of opened and closed accounts. Lenders want to see that you've used a variety of credit accounts responsibly, so anything *over* ten or fifteen credit cards is actually phenomenal. I have sixteen accounts at the time of writing this.

Keep in mind that this doesn't mean you should be maxing out all of these accounts, but you should be keeping them open.

When it comes to hard inquiries, this one is relatively simple. Your odds for approval on a credit card are impacted by how many hard inquiries you have on your account. Each time a credit card company checks your credit score, this is known as a hard inquiry. They can stay on your report for up to two years, but their effect on your number decreases significantly after six months.

Credit card companies want to see that you have few to no inquiries.

Now, I know what you might be thinking, how can I take out so many credit cards yet still keep this number low? It's really a game of balancing your cards out so that you don't apply for a whole bunch more until after that two-year period has passed.

Your credit score will be important to you throughout this whole process, so be sure to keep an eye on where it is from month to month.

Chapter 6:
Increasing/Decreasing Your
Credit Score

After all this talk about what affects your credit score, you're probably trying to figure out how to increase your score as quickly as possible.

Slow down, tiger, as this process is more of a turtle-and-the-hare-type event. You really want to do this slowly over time. It took me about three to four years to have the ultimate score of 825, which is near perfect.

This doesn't mean that you can't travel hack right away, but it's important to keep in the back of your mind, that this process happens over a long time.

How to increase your credit score

So, how can you increase your credit score? What are some of the easiest ways to get the number up quickly?

Here are several simple ways you can manage your score:

1. Pay close attention to your credit card balances each month.
   a. Make sure that you aren't using a high percentage (>30%) and pay off the balance each month.
2. Eliminate balances entirely.
   a. I was talking to a friend about how he had a $600 balance on one of his cards and I asked him if he had the money to pay it off. He told me he did, but he didn't want to spend it all right away. Then I broke down the numbers for him and showed him how much more money he would be paying the credit card company in interest. He agreed it was best to pay it off immediately.
3. Leave old debt on your report.
   a. I discovered this helpful tip from bankrate.com. They talked about how some people try to have car loans or home loans removed from their credit report the second they're paid off. But these are actually forms of good debt and prove that you're trustworthy in paying off your bills. As bankrate.com puts it, "Trying to get rid of old good debt is like making straight A's in high school and trying to expunge the record 20 years later... You never want that stuff to come off your history."
4. Bundle your credit hits together
   a. If you're shopping around for loans and have multiple hits to your credit score coming in, try to get them to happen in a very close time frame. This way, when they fall off your score two years later, they'll all come off at once instead of needing to wait a few months in between each one disappearing.

5. Pay bills on time.
   a. This seems easy and most logical, but many people just don't do it. Don't pay your bills late. Just don't. Don't buy things you can't afford. One of the biggest pieces to a good credit score is on-time payments.
6. Don't micro-manage.
   a. Your credit score will change constantly. It goes up and down and sideways. There's no need to check it every day. Once a month is fine. We already have enough stress in our lives, and if you're following the basic rules in this book, you could be like me and not need to check at all.

How to decrease your credit score

We talked about all of the factors that negatively impact your credit score, and it should seem pretty obvious right now. Your score can decrease for a number of things:

- If you applied for a line of credit recently
- If you spend more on a credit card in the past month and didn't pay it off
- If you had a late payment

The list goes on and on. It's safe to say that, by now, you know how to make your score go up, and the opposite of those actions will make it go down.

You're a smart cookie, so I believe you have a good grasp of this by now!

Chapter 7: Recovering Your Score (From Divorce, Bankruptcy, or Collections)

I understand that not everyone will have such pristine circumstances when it comes to their finances, and this is okay! It's a part of life to run into hard times, have trouble paying bills, and, for some, to have downright bad luck.

Does this mean you can't travel hack? Absolutely not! You totally can, but it may take you longer to recover your credit score before you can leverage the right deals.

For starters, one of the best ways to leverage travel hacking while you're repairing your score is to work with a friend, family member, or companion through the steps listed in this book. Have them apply for a card such as the Chase Southwest Airlines credit card and leverage their Rapid Rewards program to earn a companion pass.

Once someone has a companion pass, they can claim you as their companion, and anywhere that they fly, you too can fly for free.

So don't get discouraged if it takes you a little bit longer to get your first free flight. There are always workarounds and options.

I'll talk more about the companion pass and how you can get it when we discuss applying for your first deal. But first, I want to explain a little bit more about improving your score if you went through a divorce or bankruptcy or if you're dealing with collections.

Check your report for errors

So, for starters, you can check your credit report absolutely free once every twelve months. You'll want to get a free copy from each of the leading consumer reporting agencies – Equifax, Experian, and TransUnion.

Be sure to take advantage of this opportunity because most people don't do this. You can get a copy of your report by contacting the companies mentioned above individually or go to www.annualcreditreport.com to get it for free once per year.

Keep in mind that this is the only trusted place to do this, so don't pay another website or organization to get a copy of your report.

The goal here is to look for errors. I've seen people discover that a family member took out loans or credit cards in their name years ago, and they wouldn't have found out until it came time to buy a home.

If there are things that have been paid but still show up as a collection account, or you find an old judgment or lien you thought was paid off, be sure to take care of it right away.

Don't Borrow Money You Don't Need

It doesn't take much.

A few late payments to the mortgage company, a forgotten gas card bill, and, suddenly, your once stellar credit rating has plummeted back down the drain.

It's far too common in our economy today to fall behind on your debt and payments.

There were nearly half a million Chapter 7 bankruptcy filings in 2016. Fortunately, it decreased from the prior year, but the last thing you want to become is another statistic.

Believe it or not, just a few missed payments on a credit card can destroy your credit score for a long time. This makes it a lot harder to borrow money or, in our terms, take out a credit card and get rewards points.

The good news is that you can change this. You can break the cycle and fix your score (and your freedom).

For starters, make every payment on time. It's one of the most, if not *the* most important factors to increase (and maintain) a good score. Roughly 35% of your entire score is determined from payment history alone.

Another tip: if you can't afford the minimum payment by the due date on the card, but you'll have the money in a few days, pay it the next week. Don't wait until the next month to double your payment. It means you're thirty days late rather than a week.

Call Your Creditors

Another thing to do is reach out to your credit card companies... immediately.

If you know that you're going to have trouble making your monthly payments, it's better to call them and see what options you have rather than wait until it gets worse.

Yes, there are debt resolution services that will consolidate your credit among other things, but I live by the mantra that it's best to go straight to the source no matter how painful it may be to face.

If you do consider a debt settlement company, keep in mind that you could incur additional fines, an additional two to three years of fees and penalties, and a huge negative impact on your credit score.

But when you call your credit card company on your own, ask for a manager. The person who first answers the phone usually won't be able to help you. Let the manager know you're having money problems, and take it from there.

We've all been in this situation before on the phone with support and we get transferred around a million times only to end up back where we started. So again, go straight to the source – the person who can do something about it.

In many cases, you'll speak with someone who will work with you to establish a lower monthly payment plan, freeze the interest owed, or forgive some of your debt altogether.

Nearly every credit card company would rather get a portion of your money to pay off the debt rather than nothing at all. The last thing they want to do is take you to court.

Pay Off Your Balances

I know this one is going to hurt, but the next step is you have to pay off your balances. You also can't bring on any more debt.

If you have multiple cards, send in as much as you can to the highest interest rate balances and continue to make minimum payments on the other cards.

Leverage the debt-snowball method in paying off your cards. The debt-snowball method is a debt reduction strategy. Wikipedia claims it as being "whereby one who owes on more than one account pays off the accounts starting with the smallest balances first, while paying the minimum payment on larger debts. Once the smallest debt is paid off, one proceeds to the next slightly larger small debt above that..."

Occasionally, people compare this to the debt stacking or debt avalanche method, in which someone pays off the accounts with the highest interest rate first.

Here's a comparison between the two methods. Some think you should work on the smallest balance because, psychologically, you'll get a boost paying it off. This is the snowball concept. Then there's debt stacking, which involves putting most of your effort into the debt with the highest interest rate, since it's technically costing you more month after month.

Here are some example scenarios I'm borrowing from SavvyMoney (https://www.savvymoney.com/blog/debt/debt-stacking-vs-snowball/)

If you have four credit cards:

1) $5,000 balance at 28.9% interest
2) $700 balance at 24.9% interest
3) $2,000 balance at 11.9% interest
4) $400 balance at 17% interest

And you put $245 per month towards paying off the bills plus an additional $55 to pay off your balance faster, here's how it plays out using the Snowball Method

Priority	Balance	Minimum Payment	1st payment with this strategy	Total Interest Paid	Paid Off In
Card #1 (28.9% APR)	$5,000	$170	$170	$3141.27	37 months
Card #2 (24.9%APR)	$700	$20	$20	$150.05	13 months
Card #3 (11.9% APR)	$2,000	$40	$40	$386.81	26 months
Card $4 (17% APR)	$400	$15	$15+$55	$20.80	6 months

According to SavvyMoney, you'll be paying a total of $3,698.93 in interest charges.

Compare this to using Debt Stacking where you pay off the highest interest rates first and make a minimum payment on all others:

Priority	Balance	Minimum Payment	1st payment with this strategy	Total Interest Paid	Paid Off In
Card #1 (28.9% APR)	$5,000	$170	$170+$55	$2,283.02	31 months
Card #2 (24.9%APR)	$700	$20	$20	$388.16	32 months
Card #3 (11.9% APR)	$2,000	$40	$40	$577.45	36 months
Card $4 (17% APR)	$400	$15	$15	$105.79	31 months

If you were to use Debt Stacking, you'd pay $3,354.42 in interest charges, which saves you $350 and gets rid of your debt faster.

They mention that there are other factors to include other than simply time and money such as your motivation and overall sense of accomplishment. The Snowball Method gives you the opportunity to close out cards with annual fees and boost your credit score in the process.

I try to recommend a mix between the two to help get you debt-free sooner, but, in the end, you'll need to do some math to see the real numbers. Check out http://undebt.it for a free Debt Snowball Payment Calculator to help you crunch the numbers.

When you bring just one card down to zero debt, you instantly become more creditworthy.

More Steps

Start using cash!

Don't use credit until you've got your financials in order because, clearly, up until this point, using it has only dug you into a hole.

One of the other reasons I recommend cash is because you actually see it leave your hand, and it triggers more thrift. It's easy to swipe a card, but it's hard to whip out a crisp fifty and fork it over.

This will help you keep track of how much you're spending daily.

Another strategy I discovered is putting your credit cards in a container of water and storing them in the freezer. It's pretty hard to use your credit when it's literally frozen in a block of ice. But if you don't feel like going through the trouble, simply give your cards to a trusted relative or friend who has no problem locking the cards up and saying no.

If all else fails, cut the cards up. You'll get new ones in the mail anyway close to the expiration date, and if you need to, they'll always send you a new one for free in the mail. Just tell the company you lost your card.

Create a Budget

When my significant other graduated college with more debt than I feel comfortable mentioning, she needed to make a plan.

One of the first things I had her do was get a free account on Mint.com where she could make a budget. Everything from coffee to gas was tracked. She could see, at the end of each week, where she was overspending and where she needed to reallocate funds.

The best advice I can give to anyone, even if they have good credit, is to check where their money is going.

I have another friend who's in the habit of paying bills every month without checking them. He went six months before he realized he was paying an extra $60 a month for an international data plan! He had only gone out of the country for a two-week trip, but they never took it off his account.

Let me be totally clear - there are plenty of ways to find more money in your budget to pay off debt and clean up your credit.

The pumpkin spice latte you get three times a week in the fall? Those add up.

Stop paying more on your cell phone bill when you don't need to. Get rid of your cable TV service and just go with Internet and Netflix. Take lunch to work instead of buying it. In my house, we spend Sunday nights together meal prepping. Almost every meal is made and ready for the week to grab and go. Is it boring? Yes. Does it allow us to pay our bills down and take vacations when we want? Absolutely.

Like I said earlier, a poor credit rating isn't etched in stone. I've increased my score nearly 200 points in the last two years. You can do this too.

It's going to be odd to put yourself on a financial diet to eliminate debt, but you'll raise your credit score considerably. You'll also reduce the amount of interest you pay every month (i.e., money you never would have owed in the first place if you had paid on time).

Chapter 8: How to Track Your Credit Score for Free

Free Reports Every Twelve Months

For those who skipped over the lesson on credit, it's plain and simple. You have a right to receive your credit report absolutely free from all three bureaus once every twelve months, and you should.

Head on over to www.annualcreditreport.com to do so!

Credit Cards

Your free credit report doesn't come with a free credit score. However, in many cases, you can get a free credit score through your credit card's online login system. In most cases, all you need to do is login as if you were paying your bill and you'll be provided with a free score.

Be sure to check with your credit card coming or keep an eye out for offers in which a new credit card might provide a free report.

Credit Karma

Credit Karma is another super useful app that I recommend all my friends place on their phones. It does what's called a "soft pull," meaning it doesn't impact your credit score but it updates regularly with a rough estimate of your average score.

It's still a great free way to keep track of how much you owe on each credit card or loan, make sure no one took out a loan without your knowledge, and know, at a glance, where you stand on all six credit score factors.

Head on over to www.creditkarma.com to sign up – it's absolutely free. They try to get you to sign up for cards, but you want to be selective, which I discuss in the next chapter.

Chapter 9: Finding the Best Credit Card for Your Score

One of the first questions I get from anyone interested in travel hacking is, "How do I know what card to go for first?" I usually respond, "It depends on what you want to achieve." But the more important question to ask is, "What credit cards am I more likely to get approved for, given my credit score?"

You see, many credit card companies offer a range of cards from the free/no annual fee cards (read "high interest if you don't pay your bill" cards), which are typically meant for those with lower scores, to the ultimate "pièce de résistance" American Express Black Card (also known as the Centurion).

The black card is only for those spending beaucoup bucks, and, while it's something we can all aspire to gain, it won't be necessary for our travel-hacking purposes.

If you're looking for the best credit card for your credit score, the one place I recommend checking is NerdWallet.com where each of the most popular and active credit cards are listed. Alongside each card, you'll see the benefits, intro and regular APR, annual fee, and, most importantly, the "recommended credit score." *Recommended* being the key word here because you're not guaranteed a credit card. Banks don't owe you anything, but, as we've mentioned before, the better your credit score is, the easier this will be.

My rule of thumb is that if your score is less than 700-750 it's really not worth applying for any credit cards because a score in this range is good but not excellent.

This can be from a number of things whether you haven't had a line of credit for very long or you very recently took out loans, cards, or bought a car.

Either way, I believe that if you're anywhere higher than a 750 score you should be okay applying for most credit cards.

If you've read up until this point, applied for a credit card, but were denied, you'll want to read the chapter about what to do if your application is denied.

Later in the book, I'll share a story about getting denied originally but making a phone call and getting approved for two cards in a matter of minutes.

In summary, when it comes to finding which credit card is best for you, the rule of thumb is over 750 and you're safe for most cards, but at the end of the day, the higher the score, the better.

Chapter 10: Warning - Pay Your Bills

This warning deserves an entire chapter because it's very important. A lot of people look at what I do as an opportunity to get free stuff. Bear in mind that with great power comes great responsibility (thanks Spiderman). Thus, great lines of credit come with the responsibility to pay off your debt.

Credit cards are not toys; they're tools that, if used wisely, can be the difference between affording nice things (and being rewarded with nice things) and having nothing at all. The last thing you want is creditors calling you at all hours.

So, this is my warning, and I'm spending an entire chapter to make sure you understand this.

Pay your bills on time. Pay your balances in full every month. Don't go into debt for rewards.

I repeat.

This is my disclaimer. The strategies discussed in this book are as accurate as I can possibly state at the time of writing this book. However, times change, rules change, and I cannot be held liable or responsible for your actions and financial decisions.

It's up to you to decide what you do with your credit, financial situation, and life.

I'm simply providing a guide from my own experiences that have allowed me to live a pretty amazing life of free travel (and great credit).

I do my best in this book to provide you with the most accurate information, but the responsibility falls on you to research this more and learn more before taking action.

Travel hacking may not be right for you. Some people don't have the self-control or the patience to pull this off, and that's okay. They'll find other ways to travel the world – there's nothing wrong with paying for flights like everyone else.

I'm someone who enjoys loopholes and likes exploiting opportunities that are so abundantly available. This is what has worked in my life but may not work for you.

Nevertheless, this can be a very rewarding process, so if you feel that you're still up for the challenge, keep reading!

Chapter 11: How to Pay Off Debt Faster

Let's have an honest talk about debt. Most people have debt in some form or another.

For example, if you have a car loan, you technically have debt. Could you pay it all off tomorrow? That might be possible, but you'd be wiping out your savings, and most people like to pay a couple hundred bucks a month instead of twenty thousand dollars at once.

Here are some of the best methods for paying down your debt faster because you'll need to do this before you start racking up credit cards.

Strategy #1: Pay More Than the Minimum Payment

Most people with credit card debt are simply paying the minimum monthly payment because that's what they tell you to do (and that's what they want you to do). But if you carry a balance of roughly $15,609, and you're paying a typical 15% APR, and make the minimum monthly payment of $625, it will take you over thirteen years to pay it off. That's only if you don't increase that balance by purchasing more things.

Whether you're carrying credit card debt, personal loans, or student loans, one of the best ways to pay them all down sooner is to pay more than the required monthly minimum.

Doing so will not only help you save on interest throughout the life of your loan but also speed up the payoff process. To avoid any headaches, make sure your loan doesn't charge any prepayment penalties before you get started.

You can easily accomplish this by calling your credit card's help line and ask a representative.

Strategy #2: Try the debt snowball method.

If you're in a good place financially and feel comfortable paying more than the minimum requirement, you could start using the snowball method. This speeds the process up even more and allows you to pay off debt even faster.

As a first step, you'll want to list all of the debts you owe from smallest to largest. Go ahead; I'll wait.

Seriously, grab a piece of paper and go through everything you owe. I know this can seem daunting and even induce some anxiety but you have to face the truth sooner or later.

Then you'll want to throw all of your excess money at the smallest balance, while making the minimum payments on all of your larger loans.

Once the smallest balance is paid off, start putting that extra money toward the next smallest debt until you pay that one off, and so on.

Over time, your small balances should disappear one by one, freeing up more dollars to throw at your larger debts and loans.

This "snowball effect" allows you to pay down smaller balances first, which can feel like a huge win and further encourages you to keep it up.

This also allows you to save the largest loans for last. Ultimately, the goal is snowballing all of your extra dollars toward your debts until they're demolished, and you're finally debt-free.

Strategy #3: Pick up a side hustle.

Leveraging the debt snowball method will speed up the process, but earning more money can accelerate your efforts even further. Nearly everyone has a talent or skill they can monetize, whether it's babysitting, mowing yards, cleaning houses, or becoming a virtual assistant.

With freelancing sites like Guru.com, Fiverr.com, TaskRabbit.com, and Upwork.com, there really is no excuse for making extra cash in your spare time. The key is taking any extra money you earn and using it to pay off loans right away.

If you're looking for some ideas, check out my friend Nick Loper and his popular side hustle blog at https://www.sidehustlenation.com/. Nick uses himself as the test bunny for many side hustles and makes recommendations based on his results.

Strategy #4: Create (and live with) a bare-bones budget.

Now this is the part where things might get uncomfortable, but if you thrive in tough scenarios, this one is for you. If you really want to pay down debt faster, you'll need to cut your expenses as much as you can. One tool you can create and use is a bare-bones budget. With this strategy, you'll cut your expenses as low as they can go and live on as little as possible for as long as you can.

A bare-bones budget will look different for everyone, but be sure to leave out extracurriculars like going out to eat, cable TV, or unnecessary spending.

While you're living on a strict budget, you should be able to pay considerably more toward your debts.
Remember, bare-bones budgets are only meant to be temporary. Once you're out of debt or a lot closer to your goal, you can start adding discretionary spending back into your monthly plan.

Strategy #5: Sell everything you don't need.

If you're looking for a way to drum up some cash quickly, it might pay to take stock of your belongings first. Most of us have stuff lying around that we rarely use and could live without if we really needed to. Why not sell your extra stuff and use the funds to pay down your debts?

I know that, for me, Facebook has been a wonderful resource for getting rid of unwanted items. From Facebook Marketplace to local buy and sell groups there are plenty of places to list your items for free. You might also find Craigslist to be a valuable, free tool to list your items and quickly get them in front of local buyers.

Otherwise, you can consider selling your items on one of the various online marketplaces like eBay or Amazon.

Strategy #6: Get a seasonal, part-time job.

One of the best parts about the holidays is that stores are always looking for flexible, seasonal workers who can keep their stores operational during the busy, festive season.

If you're willing and able, you could pick up one of these part-time jobs and earn some extra cash to use toward your debts.

Even outside of the holidays, plenty of seasonal jobs may be available. Springtime brings the need for seasonal greenhouse workers and farm jobs, while summer calls for tour operators and all types of outdoor, temporary workers from lifeguards to landscapers. Fall brings seasonal work for haunted houses, pumpkin patches, and fall harvest.

The bottom line: No matter what season it is, a temporary job without a long-term commitment could be within reach.

Strategy #7: Ask for lower interest rates on your credit cards, and negotiate other bills.

If your credit card interest rates are so high that it feels almost impossible to make headway on your balances, it's worth calling your card issuer to negotiate. Believe it or not, asking for lower interest rates is actually quite commonplace. And if you have a solid history of paying your bills on time, there's a good possibility of getting a lower interest rate.

Beyond credit card interest, several other types of bills can usually be negotiated down or eliminated as well. I found that a quick call to check on my car insurance lowered it by $600 per year. Another phone call to my cable service provider allowed me to downgrade to a plan without cable TV, since we just use Netflix and the Internet. You may find that other monthly recurring fees are for larger packages than what suits your needs or simply unnecessary altogether. Always remember, the worst anyone can say is no. And the less you pay for your fixed expenses, the more money you can throw at your debts.

Strategy #8: Consider a balance transfer.

If your credit card company won't budge on interest rates, it may be worth looking into a balance transfer. With many balance transfer offers, you can secure 0% APR for up to fifteen months, although you might need to pay a balance transfer fee of around 3% for the privilege.

At the time of writing this, Citi has a balance transfer credit card that will give you twenty-one months to pay off your debt interest free.

The Chase Slate card, on the other hand, doesn't charge a balance transfer fee for the first sixty days. Further, the card offers a 0% introductory APR on balance transfers and purchases for the first fifteen months.

If you have a credit card balance that you could feasibly pay off during that time frame, transferring the balance to a 0% introductory APR card like this one could save you money on interest while simultaneously helping you pay down debt faster.

Strategy #9: Use "found money" to pay off balances.

Most people come across some type of "found money" throughout the year. Maybe you get an annual raise, an inheritance, or bonus at work. Or maybe you count on a big, fat tax refund every spring. Whatever type of "found money" it is, it could go a long way toward helping you become debt-free.

Each time you come across any unusual sources of income, you can use those dollars to pay off a big chunk of debt. If you're doing the debt snowball method, use the money to pay down your smallest balance. And if you're left with only big balances, you can use those dollars to take a huge chunk out of whatever's left.

51

Strategy #10: Drop expensive habits.

If you're in debt and consistently coming up short each month, evaluating your habits might be the best idea yet. No matter what, it makes sense to look at the small ways you're spending money daily. That way, you can evaluate whether those purchases are worth it and come up with ways to minimize them or get rid of them.

If your expensive habit is smoking or drinking, that's an easy one; *quit*. Alcohol and tobacco do nothing for you except stand between you and your long-term goals. If your expensive habit is slightly less incendiary, such as a daily latte, restaurant lunches during work hours, or fast food, the best plan of attack is usually cutting way down with the goal of eliminating these behaviors or replacing them with something less expensive.

Strategy #11: Step away from the _____.

We're all tempted by something. For many, it might be the local mall or our favorite online store. For others, it might be driving by a favorite restaurant and wishing we could pop inside for a favorite meal. And for those with a knack for spending, having a credit card in their wallet is too much temptation to bear.

Whatever your biggest temptation is, it's best to avoid it altogether when you're paying down debt. When you're constantly tempted to spend, it can be difficult to avoid new debts, let alone pay off old ones.

So, avoid temptation wherever you can, even if that means taking a different way home, avoiding the Internet, or keeping the fridge stocked so you aren't tempted to splurge on a restaurant meal. And if you must, stash those credit cards at a family member's house so you literally can't get to them. You can always bring them back out once you're debt-free.

Chapter 12: Leveraging Credit Card Bonuses

Here's the part you've probably been waiting for. It's now time to learn how to leverage credit card bonuses and do your first "hack."

Picking your first credit card bonus

When figuring out where to start, the best question to answer is, "How much can you handle?" For me, it was simply one card and dipping my toes in the water. For you, I would recommend the same.

The first card I ever got was the Southwest Airlines Rapid Rewards Premier card from Chase. I receive 2 points for every dollar I spend on Southwest flights and 1 point for every dollar spent everywhere else. I also receive 6,000 rapid rewards (their term for skymiles) on my cardmember anniversary and no foreign transaction fees. The price for the card is $99 annually.

I love this card because I'm a very loyal Southwest customer.

I think it's a great option for those who want to travel the U.S. and some closer international destinations like Cuba or Dominican Republic.

But it ultimately comes down to what you would want. Are hotel nights more valuable to you? Are flights more important? Do you simply want cash back because you shop for everything on Amazon?

Take into consideration where you spend the most money or where you'd like to receive the most reward, and, typically, that's the best place to start.

Another reason why Southwest is a safe bet is because of their companion pass. Once you hit 110,000 points in one calendar year, you receive a companion pass. This allows you to bring a friend or loved one with you on every flight absolutely free. You simply pay the taxes, which are somewhere around $5-10.

Strategies to hit spending bonuses

For the Southwest promotion mentioned above and most other offers, you'll need to hit what's called a "spending bonus" because they don't just give awards away for free.

In the case of Southwest, I needed to spend $2,000 in the first three months of having the card open (and pay it off) in order to receive my bonus.

For some, this might appear daunting because they don't spend that much money in three months. So let's explore some creative ways that you can hit this spending bonus.

- Eating out - Ever go out with friends? Foot the bill on your card and have them give you cash or Venmo/Paypal you the money for their portion of the meal. I've easily racked up a few hundred dollars in a month doing this and both are secure payment processors. Apple has also recently released Apple Pay via text message, which is just as secure.
- Paying for rent - Some services like Plastiq or RentShare allow you to pay your rent with a credit card. This tends to come with a price because there will be processing fees. But, occasionally, the payoff is worth it.
- Pay your taxes - I discovered I could pay my quarterly taxes on a credit card and would only incur a 1.87% processing fee. Ever since, I leverage this strategy four times a year to hit more spending bonuses on credit cards.
- Buying gift cards - Do you fill up your car with gas every week? Of course you do; so go ahead and buy a few $100 gift cards for your favorite gas station because, even if you don't use them in the first three months, you'll end up spending the money anyways later in the year.
- Paying tuition payments - When I was coming up short on a new bonus, I found out one of my siblings had a student tuition payment due that would knock out my entire required spend. I simply had my parents use my credit card for it and pay me back!

- Necessities - Pay for all of your food, gas, utilities, and more on one card. Don't need a lot of food for the month? Go buy bulk food items that won't go bad such as canned goods, rice, etc. You can also prepay for gas gift cards, since you know you'll use them later on down the road.

There are many other options and these might not be the best for you, but this should get you started thinking about ways to hit your spending bonuses.

What to do once you've hit your spending bonus

Once you hit your bonus spend, stop. There's no need to continue to purchase debt on your credit card. It's time to start paying everything off immediately, and be sure you don't hold a balance into the following month.

After your bonus period is up, assuming you hit your spend, you should get your reward instantly. If you don't, call your credit card company and ask when it will be active.

For me, it was almost on the ninetieth day of having my card that I received the 60,000 Rapid Rewards Points. This was, of course, after hitting the spending requirement and paying off the total bill.

Chapter 13: Manufactured Spending

What is manufactured spending (MS)?

In simple terms, manufactured spending is the process of converting credit card spending into cash, which you can then use to pay off the credit card.

The goal is twofold:

1. meet the minimum spending requirements to get the signup bonus when you open a credit card without actually buying a lot of stuff (thus allowing you to open many cards at the same time and not struggle to complete the minimum spend on all of them),
2. generate a lot of frequent flyer miles without actually spending a lot of money.

Most people will stop at the first step because the same amount of effort would yield much higher rewards than the second step, but nothing stops you from ramping things up once you're comfortable with the process.

Let's say you want United miles, so you open the Chase United credit card that gives 1 mile per dollar on every purchase, and the signup bonus is 50k miles after $3k spend. If you MS $3k, you would receive 53k miles (3k miles from your MS and 50k miles for the signup bonus). Now if you MS another $3k, you would only receive 3k more miles. Same effort but 6% fewer miles.

Is manufactured spending a requirement for hitting the credit card bonus?

Absolutely not. Remember, in the previous chapter, we discussed some options for hitting your bonus spend.

Manufactured spending takes a lot of time, especially in order to get started (a lot of research as well as trial and error). The MS methods out there are constantly changing so you'll also need to keep yourself up-to-date. If it doesn't sound like fun, then this is probably not for you.

Will this allow me to pay my rent / mortgage with a credit card?

Yes and no. If you do this right, you'll end up with cash. Cash is fungible though, so while you could pay your rent with it if you want, you could also just pay off the credit card you used to MS in the first place.

What this means is that your rent, loan, mortgage, etc. won't be of any help here, and you don't need one of these to MS. If you do have one, you don't have to limit yourself to it when you MS. In general, I would advise to just keep your MS activities separate from whatever bills you have.

So I just go to an ATM and withdraw cash with my credit card?

No! You should never do this because it will result in cash advance fees, banks usually charge interest on withdrawals starting on the day you withdraw, and you won't get any miles from the transaction.

The goal of manufactured spending is to find ways to get cash equivalent without the transaction being considered a cash advance. There are many ways to do this and I'll introduce a few in this section, but keep in mind that, occasionally, you may make a mistake and be charged cash advance fees. If that happens, pay off your entire balance immediately and move on.

A safe way to avoid being charged cash advance fees is to ask your card issuer to reduce your cash advance limit to $0, which will cause transactions that would result in cash advance fees to be declined.

Every bank has their own policy, but this limit is *usually* independent from your credit limit and, thus, doesn't affect your credit score. Some banks won't allow you to set the cash advance limit to $0 but they'll usually allow you to reduce it to a ridiculously low amount that should do the trick (cash advance transactions higher than your cash advance limit will be declined as well).

Note that some MS methods involve transactions that initially appear as cash advance but then post as regular purchases, so if you set your cash advance limit to $0 you won't be able to use those. It's up to you to decide if it's worth the risk.

Anything else I need to know before I get started?

Yes. A few golden rules:

1. No method is 100% safe, and, while you probably won't just lose your money, it might end up being tied up for a while. This is true for every single MS method out there, and even something you've been doing for months might suddenly stop working. This means you should never invest more money than you can afford to live without. If you're going to MS $3,000, make sure you have $3,000 available in your bank account in case something goes wrong and you don't see that money back before your credit card bill is due.

2. Start small. Don't go out there and try to MS $1,000 if you've never done this before. Start with $50 and go through the entire process until you understand how this works. No amount of reading will prepare you for the real thing, so don't feel like you're a pro after spending a couple of hours researching online. Once you feel comfortable with small amounts, then you can slowly ramp things up.

3. Manufactured spending is extremely YMMV (your mileage may vary). Corporate policies, hard-coded registers, store policies, manager policies, uncooperative cashiers... What works for some won't work for others and what works one day might not work the next day. If something goes

wrong, don't make a scene or create waves. Don't ask to talk to a manager if the cashier is uncooperative; don't call the bank and complain, etc. Be inconspicuous.

Funding bank accounts with a credit card

Funding bank accounts is probably the easiest MS method out there. It's also one of the safest, though it's usually not scalable.

It's a simple process: when you open a checking account, some banks allow you to do the initial funding with a credit card. Every bank has a different policy regarding this: while most don't allow it at all, some allow it up to a nominal amount ($500, $1,000) and a few rare banks allow it up to high amounts ($15k or even $100k+). In the vast majority of cases, this is a one-off opportunity and is only available for the initial account funding. Once that's done, you can't just keep adding money to your account by charging your credit card. Also, most banks will only allow the initial funding to be made with a credit card if you open your account online.

Be careful, as some credit card issuers will treat the initial funding for some of these bank accounts as cash advance. This varies widely between credit card issuers and banks, so you'll need to find a combination that works (i.e., a bank account that won't be treated as cash advance on the credit card you want to use).

There's no way to know for sure before going through with it, so the best you can do is read data points. Doctor of Credit (www.doctorofcredit.com) has a pretty comprehensive list of bank accounts that can be funded with a credit card, including the limits and which credit cards have been reported to treat these as cash advance.

Buying gift cards

Another popular MS method is to buy Visa, MasterCard, or Amex gift cards. There are two steps: find a place to buy a gift card, and then find a way to liquidate it.

While most gift cards have activation fees, these can be offset by buying them at a store that qualifies for a category bonus on your credit card (e.g., at a grocery store using an Amex Everyday Preferred for 6% back, or at an office supply store using a Chase Ink+ for 5% back). One-time promotions can make the deal even sweeter (e.g., "$20 off when buying $300 worth of gift cards" at Staples).

Finding a store that will allow you to pay for these gift cards with a credit card can be tricky. Some stores have corporate policies against this while others simply hard-coded their registers to decline credit card payments. Even if this isn't the case, your local store could have a policy against this, or there could be an overzealous manager or an uncooperative cashier afraid of fraud.

Online research should allow you to find out which chains have hard-coded registers and corporate policies, but for the rest, you'll have to try it out yourself at your neighborhood stores.

Even if your credit card doesn't have any category bonus, some places sell gift cards with low activation fees that should easily be offset by whatever rewards you'll get from the transaction. Simon malls are a popular example as most of them sell $500 Visa gift cards with a $3.95 activation fee, so less than 1%.

These gift cards can't be used at ATMs so you'll need to find a way to liquidate them. Most Visa gift cards and some MasterCard gift cards can be configured with a PIN that will allow you to use them as debit cards. You can't do this on Amex gift cards, so these are notoriously hard to liquidate: most people just use them to buy Visa gift cards and end up liquidating these instead.

Here are a few popular ways to liquidate gift cards with a PIN:

- Buy money orders. Some grocery stores will allow you to buy a money order using a debit card (in your case, a Visa gift card) for a nominal fee, which you can then deposit in your bank account. Again, not all grocery stores will allow this and you'll need to do some online research and field testing to find one that will work. Also, be aware that some banks frown upon customers depositing many money orders, so you'll also need to research which banks are safe and which ones aren't.

- Load them onto reloadable prepaid cards such as Amex Serve. You can then use the bill pay feature to pay off the credit card you used to buy those gift cards with.

- Pay off your credit card. Some banks allow you to pay off a credit card using a debit card, and gift cards *sometimes* work. Citi and FIA (Bank of America, Fidelity Amex) are two examples.

Keep in mind this is only meant as an introduction, and it's missing a lot of details. You'll need to do a lot more research before you start going out there buying gift cards!

Reloadable prepaid cards

Some reloadable prepaid cards can be loaded with a credit card directly online, and these can usually be liquidated more easily than gift cards.

Another popular example is Amex Serve, although its usefulness has been severely limited since they stopped accepting non-Amex credit cards. You can still use an Amex credit card to load money onto it, but only third-party Amex credit cards will generate rewards from these loads.

Other MS methods

While these are probably the most popular and publicly discussed methods for manufactured spending, there are actually many more out there.

This is a touchy subject because, while you reap the rewards from manufactured spending, someone else loses money in the process (usually whoever pays for the credit card transaction fees). As a result, MS methods that start getting popular also start costing a lot of money for someone, and they end up being restricted or simply shut down. Because of this, many people won't share their MS tricks or discuss their MS methods in public.

The best way to find new MS methods is to be on the lookout for interesting opportunities and do a lot of field-testing. Being actively involved in some MS communities might also get you invited to circles that are more private with people who will share information more freely.

Where do I go for more information now?

FlyerTalk has dedicated threads for the most publicly talked about MS methods, usually with an extensive wiki. Many churning blogs also cover manufactured spending.

And, of course, Google is your friend here, so don't forget to search around for more.

Chapter 14: What to Do if Your Application Fails

If you're approved for a credit card, you'll typically find out right away. When you're denied, however, it's a completely different situation. Credit card issuers rarely tell you on the spot why your credit card application was denied.

Instead, they send a letter, an adverse action letter, within seven to ten business days of your application, which gives more details about the decision.

The adverse action letter will give you the specific reason or reasons your credit card application was denied. The letter will also include instructions for getting a free copy of your credit report if one was used in the decision.

While you're waiting to get your letter, here are some possible reasons your credit card application could be denied. If you're familiar with your credit history, you may be able to guess why your application was denied.

1. Your loan balances are too high.

If you haven't been paying down your loan balances, credit card issuers are hesitant to give you a credit card because there's a risk you may not pay that off either. Reducing your loan balances before applying for a credit card can help you get approved.

2. Your credit card balances are too high.

Credit card companies want to see that you're only using a portion of the credit available to you. If you're using too much of your available credit, especially if you're maxed out, you can count on having your credit card application denied. Keeping your balances below 30% is best for your credit score and your chances of getting approved.

3. There are too many inquiries on your credit report.

Applying for too many credit cards and loans within a short time can get your credit card application denied, regardless of whether you're approved for the other credit cards. Minimize your credit inquiries to improve your chances at getting your next credit card application approved.

4. Your income is too low.

The income required for a credit card varies by credit card issuer. Your credit card application could be denied if you don't make enough money for that particular credit card or if you don't have income of your own. Credit card issuers don't publish minimum income requirements for their credit cards, so it's up to you to estimate which credit cards fit your income.

5. You have too many credit cards.

The number of credit cards you already have can influence whether your credit card application is denied. There's no universal number that applies to all credit card applications. Instead, it varies by credit card issuer.

6. You have a recent collection or public record.

As time goes on, collections and public records affect your credit less. However, these hurt your credit the most when they first appear on your credit report. These serious delinquencies are a sign to the credit card company that you don't have enough money to meet your financial obligations.

7. Your last delinquency was too recent.

Credit card issuers look at more than just the type of delinquency. They also consider how long it's been since you were last delinquent. A ninety-day late payment from six months ago will hurt your chances of getting approved more than one from six years ago.

8. You have a charge-off on your credit report.

A charge-off is a credit card balance that went unpaid for six months or more. It's one of the worst things that can appear on your credit report. Honestly, if you failed to pay another credit card, a new credit card company will hesitate to give you a credit card. Paying the charged-off balance will improve your chances of getting approved.

9. You have a thin file or limited credit history.

You could be denied if you've never had credit before or if you don't have much experience with credit. If you don't have at least one account that's been active in the past six months, FICO can't generate a credit score for you. Without a credit score, the credit card company is more likely to deny your application. If you're just starting out with credit, consider a secured credit card or student credit card.

10. You're not old enough to get a credit card.

If you're under age 18, you'll probably have your credit card application denied because you're under the legal age to get a credit card. There are some exceptions. For example, you may be able to get approved for a credit card if you have your own income and you've already been added as an authorized user to your parents' credit card.

11. You didn't completely fill out the application.

If your application is missing vital information, such as a physical address or date of birth, you risk being denied. The good thing about most online credit card applications is that they often won't let you submit the application until it's complete. That way, you eliminate the risk of having your credit card application denied because it wasn't complete.

12. You haven't been at your current job long enough.

An unstable work history can lead to your credit card application being denied. Credit card issuers like applicants who've been on their job consistently. If you've been job-hopping and have periods of unemployment, you may have a hard time getting approved for a credit card.

Improve Your Credit Before the Next Application

The adverse action letter will include instructions for ordering a free copy of your credit report, if something on your credit report led to your application's denial. Order the credit report and review it for any errors. Dispute errors with the credit bureau if you find any. Otherwise, use this free credit report as an opportunity to repair your credit before your next credit card application.

A credit card rejection isn't a personal jab, but it can sure feel like one.

It stings to read about a part of your credit history you'd rather forget, or learn about a negative entry on your credit report from an automated message.

But as painful as rejections are, you can learn from them. Once you know why you didn't qualify, you'll be in a better position to either request a reconsideration or apply successfully for another card. Here's how you can move on in five steps.

How to recover

1. Read your adverse action notice
2. Review your credit report
3. Double-check the application
4. Ask the issuer to reconsider
5. Apply for a card you can get

1. Read your adverse action notice

There's no need to guess why your application was rejected. The Fair Credit Reporting Act requires issuers to send you an "adverse action" notice if they deny you credit because of information that appears in your credit report. And if they deny you based on income or another non-credit-related factor, they'll generally notify you about that as well.

Many banks send these notices as electronic statements immediately after you apply; others deliver the news by letter or by phone.

Reading your adverse action notice can give you a better idea of what your issuer is looking for in an applicant and how you can improve your chances of a future approval.

2. Review your credit report

Your adverse action notice might include your credit score if it was a factor in the decision. It will also remind you that you have a right to request a free copy of the credit report used in the application decision within the next sixty days.

Follow up on this offer, especially if the notice cites a negative entry in your credit reports that you didn't know about, or your score is lower than you expected. Inaccuracies are fairly common: About one out of every four consumers has errors on their credit report that might affect their score, according to a 2012 Federal Trade Commission study, the most recent information available.

Once you receive your copy, review it. If you find errors, dispute them in writing with the credit bureau. Even if you don't, that bird's-eye view of your accounts can help you find ways to improve your credit and pay off debt.

3. Double-check the application

Take a second look at the information you provided to the issuer in case you accidentally made yourself seem less creditworthy than you really are. Maybe you said your annual income was $5,000 when you meant to say $50,000. Or maybe you reported that your rent costs $6,000 per month when you meant $600.
It's not just fat-finger mistakes that can trip you up. You also need to know what counts as income.

Most issuers don't specify how applicants should report income, so some report only their own independent earnings. In fact, an amendment in the Credit Card Act of 2009 allows applicants over 21 to report any income to which they have "reasonable expectation of access." This is a big deal for a stay-at-home parent who might not earn any income. Thanks to this provision, they can report their partner's income and more easily qualify for credit.

Nerd Tip:

If you're under 21, you can report only your own independent income on a card application. This applies even with student credit cards.

If you realize you made a mistake on the application, call the issuer's customer service line. A representative might be able to amend the error and approve your application. Here are the credit card customer service lines for each major issuer:

- American Express: 800-528-4800 (click on "Contact Us" at the bottom of the American Express page for a pop-up screen with contact information)
- Bank of America®: 800-732-9194
- Barclaycard: 888-232-0780
- Capital One: 800-227-4825
- Chase: 800-432-3117
- Citi: 888-201-4523
- Discover: 800-347-2683
- U.S. Bank: 800-947-1444
- Wells Fargo: 800-869-3557

4. Ask the issuer to reconsider

At this point, you probably have a decent idea of the credit card's underwriting standards and how you missed the mark. Sometimes, it's best to accept the decision and apply for a card you're more likely to receive. But if you were close to meeting the issuer's criteria, you might want to call its customer service line and ask for a reconsideration.

Explain how you've improved your credit habits and why you'd be a good customer.

Suppose you were rejected because of a thirty-day past due payment from a few years ago. Explain how you've improved your credit habits and reassure the representative that you'll be a good customer. Remember that the representative doesn't have to honor your request. You might not be able to talk your way into a "yes," but it's worth a try.

5. Apply for a card you can get

Sometimes, applying for a different card that fits your credit profile makes the most sense:

- If you have bad credit or no credit, consider applying for a secured credit card, which is a card with cash collateral, and building up your credit by using it properly.

- If you have decent credit and are still having trouble, try another issuer. The card you end up with might not be your first choice, but if you manage the account well, it could open up other options in the future.

How I Got Denied and Accepted Minutes Later

I mentioned that, in the past, I had applied for multiple credit cards in one day and was denied. I want you to understand that no doesn't always mean no with credit card applications. Most people see the denial and fail to try again because they're not aware of the options.

One of my best travel hacks ever was to obtain the Southwest Airlines Companion Pass. Essentially, you need to fly 100 flights in one calendar year or accumulate 110,000 rewards points in one calendar year to receive a companion pass.

The companion pass allows you to bring a companion with you for free on any flight that you book until the end of the following calendar year. So, if I were to obtain the companion pass in July of 2018, I would have free flights for my companion until December 31st of 2019. This is great because some people time it so perfectly that they redeem the pass in January and have it for nearly two years!

For my attempt, I already had a Southwest Airlines Visa card for my business from when I first began travel hacking and didn't know any better, so I knew it would be tough to gain two more cards. The one in my possession was a few years old, so the points wouldn't count toward the calendar-year requirement. Fortunately, Southwest offers a Premier and a Plus version of both the business and personal credit cards. This means that there are four credit cards with the chance of getting the companion pass twice, assuming you're approved for all four cards.

If you play your cards right (get it?) you can get the companion pass for two years, then take out two additional cards and receive the pass for an additional two years. Alternatively, you could cancel your credit cards after your pass has expired and, a year or two later, apply once again and restart the process. This is, of course, frowned upon and does impact your credit score, so it's not ideal.

My best option was to apply for both personal cards, as I found out they would be easier to obtain. I applied for both the Personal Premier and Personal Plus cards when a 60,000 point reward opportunity came up. I was quickly notified that my application would require further processing and that I would receive a notification within 7-14 days via snail mail. I thought to myself perhaps I could get the other card, so I applied for that one as well within the same hour and received the same notice.

At first, this was disappointing, but then I started to do some research. I realized that when I applied, I used Baltimore as my city when, in reality, my city as listed by the postal service is technically Pikesville. In the past, this has never been an issue, but, for whatever reason, the credit card company had to go with the city on file.

So I began my call to the reconsideration line or what people call the "recon" line for Chase, the card issuer. I finally got someone on the phone and simply told them what had happened. They said I could send over a copy of my driver's license to fix the issue and that I would be approved. I thought things were all fine and dandy until I asked about the second denial. The representative said that because I had applied for two cards in one day, their system automatically flagged me, thinking I could be a fraudster, and she asked why I needed two cards.

Again, from my research, I learned that if you explain to the recon representative that you'd like to separate expenses into personal and business, then it would be much more likely to get pushed through. I stated my case by telling them I worked with a nonprofit and wanted to separate my expenses between cards. After a brief hold, I was approved!

To be fair, I don't have expenses for the nonprofit that I place on a credit card, as everything is done via a debit card or check. However, I could have told them anything such as I'm planning a wedding and have some large expenses that I want separate from my everyday spending. There are a multitude of explanations you can give, but the point to make is that you don't want to appear as if you're purposely gaming the system; otherwise, the representative will be less likely to push your application through.

In the end, this was a huge win for me and my companion, as we've been able to use the 120,000 free Rapid Rewards points gained from getting accepted for two 60k credit applications. It's important to note that you cannot get one card, have your spouse get one, and attempt to use the same Rapid Rewards account. It must be the same person and account applying for both cards.

If you want a simple-to-use chart that explains what you should do if a credit card application is denied, check out this handy resource from a helpful Redditor at http://www.zephanmoses.com/creditrecon

Chapter 15: Canceling Credit Cards

A lot of people think that cancelling a credit card is a good thing, but this couldn't be further from the truth. Remember when we talked about how your credit score is calculated?

Your score will be higher with more lines of open credit. It boils down to how much of that credit you're using that negatively impacts you.

So when should you cancel a credit card and what do you gain from doing so?

Truthfully, you gain very little from closing out an account. If a credit card isn't charging you an annual fee, you really have no reason to close it.

It will continue to build your credit score and has no negative impact on you whatsoever, assuming it has no remaining balance.

In the case of the Chase Southwest Rapid Rewards credit cards, you actually gain more points by keeping the card open each year. The only downside is this particular card does come with an annual fee.

The bottom line is, unless you have multiple cards open that are hurting you with annual fees, there's really no reason to close a credit card. If anything, pull it out every once in a while to buy a candy bar or gas and pay it off just so the company sees it being as active every few months.

Outside of that, I recommend leaving your credit cards that hold a zero balance and are not in use somewhere safe where you won't touch them. It can't hurt to log in each month just to make sure you don't have any unforeseen charges, but you don't need the card in hand to do so.

Chapter 16: How to Find the Best Domestic Flights

We've covered pretty much everything you need to know about getting your credit score up, and we've reviewed the top methods for taking out credit cards and hitting the spending bonuses. It's time to figure out where the best flights come from within the U.S.

Don't worry; we'll talk about international flights later, but, as you might have suspected, I'm a huge fan of Southwest Airlines.

My first answer when it comes to finding the best domestic flights is using the airline where you have the most points.

For obvious reasons, you'll save the most money on flights that you can redeem points for. But there are a few really good strategies for discovering cheap flights.

Google Flights/ITA Matrix

The ITA Matrix is owned by Google and is an airfare search engine that crunches all the numbers put out by some of the top airline carriers so that you can find the best flights by price and even consider some options that the typical airline website won't let you take advantage of.

Some people go to Priceline, Kayak, or Travelocity, thinking those sites have their best interest in mind. But, at the end of the day, those sites need to make money, whereas Google isn't really concerned with that.

The ITA Matrix is an all-in-one search engine for flights that looks at different routes, prices, and options for most of the top airlines.

Originally created in 1996 by MIT scientists, the ITA Matrix is also used for Google Flights, so if you've ever used the Flights feature, you've already seen ITA at work.

Simply head on over to https://matrix.itasoftware.com/ and you'll be able to compare things like cost per mile, geographic search, an interactive calendar, filters, and color-coded searches based on length of trip.

The ITA Matrix is usually my first stop when I'm searching for prices, although one thing to consider is they don't display Southwest Airline flights and a few other airlines, so you always want to do your research.

Deals and Errors

Another great way to find a cheap flight is by paying attention to cheap airfare websites like The Flight Deal (https://www.theflightdeal.com/) or Secret Flying (http://www.secretflying.com/) among many others.

These websites are quick to post deals that pop up. Some of these offers may only be available for an hour, day or week, so be sure to sign up for notifications from them or, at least, check their site every now and again.

These sites also post about airline ticket errors. With thousands of flights each day being controlled and priced by computers, they're bound to slip up.

Errors in flight prices or different combinations of flights can be a great way to land a deal. The only downside is you typically have to make your calendar available at very odd times. So, this isn't the most effective method for someone who works the typical nine-to-five job.

Sales

This strategy is pretty cut and dry. Airlines run sales for holidays, the new year, or anything in between.

One of the best ways to find out when these sales go live is to subscribe to their email promotions and to check the special offers section of each major airline from time to time. Again, most of your favorite travel blogs will announce when these happen as well.

Advance Booking

I've seen strategies online that mention things like a certain "golden" timeframe to book your flight or things like, "only book your flight on Tuesday after 3pm because that's when airlines update their prices."

Some of these are true to an extent, but no one has found a surefire way to get a good price on a flight. My best advice for you is to book in advance. I've had too many friends ask about wanting to book a flight a few weeks out and they want to know where to find a good price. Truthfully, you won't, and there's not a whole lot that can be done. Plan well in advance, and you'll see a decrease in price for looking ahead.

Low-Fare Airlines

I've always been against budget airlines such as Spirit or Frontier mostly because of their poor customer service records and the fact that they nickel and dime you for everything. I believe that charging to bring a carry-on bag on a plane is quite ridiculous. You're on a plane; why wouldn't you just include the fee in the ticket? No one gets on a plane without a bag.

But if you're a no-frills kind of person and you're willing to pack super light, then these airlines might be for you. They also might be good options for a quick weekend trip or hopping a couple of states over rather than driving.

Personally, I'll never fly on these airlines because I've heard too many horror stories, including cancelled flights and missed connections, but to each their own. If the price is right, it might not be the worst thing.

Summary

Ultimately, what it comes down to is that there's no exact equation to finding the best price for a flight. Prices fluctuate daily and, sometimes, hourly, so it makes sense that you'd want to have as many points on hand to cover the cost, whatever that may be.

You can try little tricks like using an Incognito or "Private" browsing tab. According to *Today Show,* fifty to one hundred days prior to takeoff is the best time before fares start going up and seats start selling. But who's to say a holiday pricing special won't come around a week beforehand? It happens all the time.

The best way to search for good prices is using the ITA Matrix and then cross-comparing with other airlines that aren't listed in the search. From there, take into account which airlines you have (or receive) points for and go from there.

Chapter 17: How to Find the Best International Flights

Depending on where in the United States you live, you may find it easier and cheaper to travel. It helps to live near a big international hub like New York or Chicago.

Some up-and-coming budget international airlines like WOWAIR offered $99 flights from Washington DC to Europe when they first got started.

WOWAIR is a great company because they set up a transfer point in Reykjavik, Iceland. What this means is that all of their flights stop in Iceland and the best part is you can stop there for as long as you'd like then transfer over to your final destination!

You can find out more at https://wowair.us/, but let's dive into some of the best ways to find international flights.

Tweets

This might sound crazy, but low fares pop up all the time on Twitter, so even if you aren't social-media savvy, it might be worth getting an account to follow your favorite airlines (and blogs).

One of the techniques I recommend is to set up a Twitter alert for certain search terms like *flight, deal, airline,* and *sale.* That way, you can get an email alert any time something new comes out. Websites like https://warble.co/ will help you send alerts straight to your email inbox!

Fare Alerts

Along the same lines as Twitter alerts are regular alerts from websites. Blogs such as AirFareWatchDog (https://www.airfarewatchdog.com/), The Hopper (https://www.hopper.com/), SkyScanner (https://www.skyscanner.com/) and many others allow you to sign up for email alerts for flight deals. This also applies for domestic flights but comes in handy much more for international trips.

Buy Late

I know this contradicts everything I said in the previous chapter, but there are some advantages to buying last minute! Some sites such as Last Minute Travel (https://www.lastminutetravel.com/) will help you search airline websites for last minute flight deals. If you can deal with a flexible itinerary and dates, this could be a fantastic money-saving option for you. It's not ideal and doesn't work for most, but, for a few, this is gold.

Just Buy

One of the hardest parts about looking for a cheap flight is knowing when it's time to stop looking around and just buy the ticket.

Could the flight increase in price within 24 hours? Absolutely. Could it decrease, too? Yes, but what about missing out on a flight entirely because you waited for the perfect deal but never pulled the trigger.

Sometimes, it's best to just make the purchase and stop looking.

Refunds & Credits

If you use a website like Orbitz.com who has a Best Price Guarantee, then you're entitled to get money back if you find your itinerary for less on another website.

But what's even better is getting bumped from a flight. Most people who are on an international flight don't want to wait to take the next hop across the pond. But airlines can offer you a pretty penny if they accidentally overbooked.

If your schedule allows for it, take the few hundred extra bucks or free flight credits to get on the next flight. Sometimes, airlines will compensate for hotel stay as well.

This can be a great way to get free travel for the next trip!

Location

Despite the fact that my hometown is Baltimore and I live twenty minutes driving from Baltimore Washington International Airport, it can be cheaper to buy a $30 megabus ticket to New York and fly out of one of the airports there, or even take the Amtrak train down to Washington, DC and fly out of their airports.

The same goes for a destination. If I'm flying to San Francisco, perhaps I can take a different route and fly into Oakland, get a rental car and make the drive. It's always worth it to look at other nearby airports or travel opportunities.

I realize this might be uncomfortable to some, but the truth about travel "hacking" is that you aren't really hacking the system; you're hacking your own flexibility and ability to travel.

Chapter 18: Hotel Hacks

One of the easiest ways to get hotel points is to take out a credit card with your favorite hotel chain. For example, I stay with Holiday Inn a lot, so, for me, it made sense to take out the IHG rewards card, which allows me to stay at any number of hotels within their network. I've also heard great things about the Marriott Rewards credit cards, which make huge bonus offers a couple times per year.

In this chapter, I wanted to focus more on how to leverage staying in a hotel rather than credit card deals, since you've probably figured out the basics from previous chapters. Hotel points are very similar to airlines, so there isn't a whole lot to explain that wouldn't be redundant.

However, here are some hotel "hacks" that you can deploy while you're at it!

1. Book your room and flight together
    a. Oftentimes, you'll book a flight through Southwest's online portal and it will ask if you need to book anything else such as a hotel or a

rental car. This is also a feature of websites like Priceline, Travelocity, and more. There can be a catch, so be sure to read the fine print. More often than not, you'll need to pay everything in advance. There also might be additional stipulations regarding cancellations or changes, so be careful.

2. AAA discounts
   a. If you aren't already a member of AAA, the discounts and benefits alone can be worth the membership fee. It doesn't just apply to hotels but I've leveraged having AAA for rental car prices and more. AAA also has a great feature for drivers under the age of twenty-five. In most areas, you cannot rent a car until you're twenty-five years old; otherwise, companies will slap you with a large fee. But with AAA, you can bypass this!

3. Up your status
   a. Once you've chosen your loyalty to a hotel chain, they want to keep you there, which is exactly why they create status programs that offer things like early check-in, late checkout, free breakfast, room upgrades, and more. Be sure to take advantage of this because it's free! The more you stay with that hotel chain, the better.

4. Extended stay
   a. If you're staying somewhere longer than a week, try calling the hotel instead of booking online to see if they can give you a discount. Sometimes, you can negotiate a better rate than what's on the website or deal sites.

5. Book during the off-season

a. This one is pretty obvious, but prices will be cheaper during the off-season so you can save beaucoup bucks.

6. Book direct

a. A lot of people love the comfort and ease of booking online but it's worth making the phone call to the hotel and asking, "Is that the best you can give me?" Most online systems are highly automated and don't have a knack for sympathy. Talking to a real person and asking what they can do for you makes all the difference. If you're having a special celebration like an 80th birthday, anniversary, or graduation, be sure to mention this on the call. Hotels have gone to great lengths for me to leave notes, chocolates, or little surprises to celebrate the occasion.

7. Private browsing

a. I rarely do this, but I've heard mixed reviews on using a private or incognito browsing tab on your computer because it makes it much harder for websites to track where you've been and what you've looked at. From time to time, prices will be cheaper especially if you book a hotel through its foreign website.

8. Review your stay

a. Offering to write a 5-star review on websites like Yelp, Trip Advisor, or even tweeting it to your audience can be the difference between hundreds of dollars a night and more affordable rooms. I've played twitter battles before with multiple hotels in Boston, getting them to fight to give me the best price by simply tweeting where I want to stay, tagging each of the hotels, and asking who could accommodate me.

9. BYOF
   a. I've gone on business trips when I knew that I'd be stuck in a hotel for three or four days at a time. I don't like being forced to eat hotel food for such a long period because A) it's not healthy and B) it's usually expensive. So, I make it a point to stop at a local Trader Joes or Whole Foods and stock up on food I can cook between the microwave and utensils in my room.

10. Ask
    a. A lot of my friends forget to do this. The power of asking is crucial. It doesn't have to be fancy but if you don't ask, you don't get. Ask if you can get a break on the room price or get free Wi-Fi or other premium amenities included. In the past, I've gotten free breakfast vouchers.

11. Bring an HDMI cable
    a. HDMI cables are cheap but also allow you to connect your laptop to the TV. Why flip through a bunch of channels you don't know when you can use the free Wi-Fi to stream your favorite Netflix show to the TV? This is also great if you're working in your hotel room. Why work on a 13-inch screen when you can have the whole 40-inch TV!?

12. Email the manager
    a. If you email the general manager of a hotel and let them know that last time you stayed in their hotel you had a mediocre experience, the GM may try to build a relationship with you and get

your business back by offering to waive resort fees, upgrading rooms, and more.

13. Groupon & last-minute deals
    a. One of the best vacations I ever took was a three-hour drive away to a casino and resort on a beautiful lake. It was a fantastic weekend getaway and all thanks to Groupon. We saved a ton of money, got free vouchers for the casino, and went boating on the lake. Don't forget to check apps like Hotel Tonight for last-minute deals.

14. Check the lost and found
    a. Did you forget a charger? Perhaps you need some other cable for your computer? Check the lost and found. Hotels usually have a drawer full of chargers and accessories that people have left behind.

15. Use the do not disturb sign
    a. I routinely use the do not disturb sign because if I really need my bed made, I'll make it myself. There's no need for housekeeping to come into my room where I may be keeping a laptop or other valuables.

16. Power The Room
    a. I found this was more common in Europe, but a lot of hotels are using your key card as a way to turn on power to the room. If you want to leave the AC on while you're gone, simply place an expired gift card or room key card in the slot to keep the electricity running.

17. Leave Notes
    a. If you do have someone come in to clean your room during the day, use the pen and pad that most hotels leave to write a nice letter to

housekeeping. After all, they never really interact with guests and are working long hours. I've found that this little act of kindness means getting extra shampoos or coffee. It's worth it and only takes an extra minute.

Chapter 19: Hack Your Pack - Traveling Light

Traveling light can mean the difference between an aching back and wallet by the end of your trip and being at ease with less. I wanted to cover a few tips on how you can pack lighter and still bring everything that you need.

- Use dryer sheets or the hotel bar of soap to keep your dirty laundry bag smell under control.
- Put a moisturizer on before your overnight flights to wake up feeling more refreshed.
- Pack items like a laptop in smaller bags so you have options when you want to take a smaller daypack out.
- Wear a heavy coat on the plane – it doubles as a pillow.
- Always put underwear in your carry on in case luggage is lost.
- Leave things behind that you can purchase when you get to your destination like toothbrush, toothpaste, toiletries, etc.

- Use a lightweight backpackers bag, such as a 25-liter backpack, instead of typical luggage.
- Don't pack more than two pairs of shoes and, if you can, keep it to one.
- If you're only traveling for a couple of days, simply bring one pair of jeans.
- Grab a portable charger for the longer hauls to keep your electronics charged.
- Functionality over fashion – if it's a vacation, there's no need for outfits; just bring what you need.
- Portable laundry detergent is great for washing your clothes in the sink; then use the hair dryer and shower rack to dry them out.
- Unless you're traveling to the Amazon rainforest, you can buy almost everything where you're going.
- Use packing cubes to compress your clothing and pack more into a small space.
- Roll your clothes; don't fold them.
- Pack what you think you need and then cut it down by 50%. Be sure to take notice of how much you really didn't need.
- Leverage empty space inside of your shoes to pack socks and underwear; it takes up less space.
- Email a copy of your passport and itinerary to yourself for easy emergency access.
- Notify your bank that you'll be traveling out of state or country so they don't bar you from taking out money from the ATM.
- Get a card like the Charles Schwab checking account debit card that reimburses you for international ATM fees.
- Pack an eye mask and earplugs for tougher nights in hostels, trains, etc.

- Download Google Maps offline so you won't need cell service to get around.
- Forgot to bring a charger? No worries, as most TVs have a USB plug in the back for powering devices. You can save space by not bringing the charger, since most hotels have a charging port on the alarm clock or TV.

There are tons of other ways you can pack lighter, and you'll learn as you go! These are just a few to get you started.

Chapter 20: The Fear of Going on the Road

When I first set off on my adventures, one of the biggest fears I had was leaving everything behind. I thought that by following where my heart desired, I was putting my business on hold and essentially saying, "If it fails, it fails."

I made a mistake by having this mentality because it was limiting.

I thought about things like…

"What if I come back to find that all of my clients have left me for a competitor?"

"What if my house burns down and I lose everything I left behind?" This actually did happen to a friend of mine, and he saw it as a huge blessing and lesson to become more minimalist.

"What if when I get back, I don't even have money to pay for rent?"

"What if I find myself in the middle of a foreign country having a panic attack for the first time in a decade, and I don't have any medication?" This happened to me in Israel.

"What if I get back and my family decides they won't support me because they don't understand my lifestyle?"

These thoughts and many others came flooding into my mind, and they might come up for you too. Let's look at the reality behind them all:

"What if I come back to find that all of my clients have left me for a competitor?"

If your clients have left you for a competitor, they must not have been very loyal to you in the first place and you'd be better off finding clients who only want to work with you.

"What if my house burns down and I lose everything I left behind?"

As I mentioned previously, my friend Josh had this happen. He owned a photography studio in Maryland and was traveling Southeast Asia for about half a year. When he found out that he had lost everything, he simply extended his trip because the cost of living was cheaper over there, so he actually saved money by not coming home.

"What if when I get back, I don't even have money to pay for rent?"

What if you get back and have to crash with a family member or a friend for a couple weeks until you get back on your feet? Don't have anyone? There are sites like www.couchsurfing.com with people all over the world willing to welcome you into their home for free.

"What if I find myself in the middle of a foreign country having a panic attack for the first time in a decade, and I don't have any medication?"

Funny enough, this happened to me. I took Dramamine to knock myself out for my 12-hour flight to Israel from New York but I didn't take enough, so I kept nodding in and out of consciousness. By the time we got to Israel, I was groggy, exhausted, and nauseous. It was the perfect storm leading to a panic attack of hyperventilation and complete loss of appetite. I felt like my body was going into shock. But the first night we were there, I found a local doctor who was able to prescribe just enough of my old medication to get me through the trip. By day three, I felt like a million bucks and didn't even need my medication anymore. Believe it or not, there are doctors in other countries ready and willing to help.

My biggest fear of all was losing my business because I felt that if I didn't have my business, I didn't have money, and if I didn't have money, I didn't have my basic needs of food and shelter. But I surprised myself, as most travelers do when they get back from their first big trip.
I didn't notice until I had gotten back home from my first "travel hack" when I took a whole month off to travel the country. I opened up my laptop, logged into my business accounting software, and saw that I had pulled off a profitable month!

But how on earth did I pull it off?

Being on the road, I realized there was a lot of down time. Whether it's sitting around an airport waiting for the next flight or simply having a day with nothing to do, there's plenty of time for work.

I own a video production business, so I thought it would be nearly impossible to work while on the road. After all, I wasn't bringing my camera gear along with me, and if I don't have equipment, I can't work.

At this time, I learned a very valuable lesson in business: the power of taking deposits.

As a freelancer, or anyone in the creative world, you have to put in a lot of work before you actually complete the project. In order to protect yourself from going unpaid, it's recommended to ask for a percentage of the total bill as a deposit. I hadn't done this until I was on the road, but I found myself receiving emails from clients who were willing to wait until I got home. They wanted to work with me and would do whatever it took.

I type this in an email to a potential client: "I'm going to be extremely busy when I get home because a lot of people have requested to work with me... I really value you as a client and it means a lot that you want to work with me. If you're willing to place a 50% deposit payment now, I can block off the dates that we'll film together, and those days will be locked down for you and only you."

This made my clients feel really special because I was showing intention up front that I would be their exclusive videographer and they would have my full attention.

I realize that this strategy won't work in every business, but this is just an example.

The main point I want to get across is that whatever fear you may have about hitting the road, taking a break, getting out of town, chances are that it really isn't true.

As I learned from Kyle Maynard, a speaker, author, and mixed martial arts athlete known for becoming the first quadruple amputee to ascend Mount Kilimanjaro, we are born with only two fears: a fear of falling and a fear of loud noises. That's it. There's literally nothing else in this world that we have an innate fear of, meaning everything else that scares us has been learned over time.

Whether you learned you hated clowns from one time as a kid going to the circus or you simply have never been around one, the fear has been created over time. This means that it can be unlearned too.

There's nothing to it but to do it.

"What if I get back and my family decides they won't support me because they don't understand my lifestyle?"

Family can be a tough subject for many people. You're raised with pressure from both sides to behave a certain way, wear certain clothes, and even become a certain type of person. In my life, this was amplified by the fact that I had stepparents and eight younger siblings. I knew I had to be a role model and set an example.

At the same time, I believe it's crucial to remain true to who you are and follow your intuition. I think there's always a chance for family to come back around, and, in my case, this was a completely ridiculous fear that never even came into play.

Just know that if you make a life decision, it has consequences. Your actions may have results that you could never foresee, so be conscious in your decisions and be sure to think things through. Consider who will be affected in the process, and if you find that you truly have nothing to lose, then I say go for it.

As Helen Keller said, "Life is either a daring adventure or nothing at all." If a girl who was born deaf and blind can become an author, lecturer, and activist, then there's no reason why you can't achieve anything in life that you set your mind to.

Chapter 21: Turning Passion Into Payment

Having the ability to get paid for the things you truly love is one of the best feelings in the world. It's as if you've found perfect serendipity in your life because you can wake up doing exactly what you want to do and you no longer have the fear of paying your bills.

As you may have learned already, when it comes to becoming debt-free, a huge burden will be lifted, but many people ask me about making money and how to do it for the rest of their lives.

Let's do a quick rewind on where my income has come from over the past five or so years.

For starters, my video production business is and pretty much always will be my main income source. I work extremely hard to build this company every day and have seen extraordinary growth for a first-time entrepreneurial pursuit. Nearly all other forms of income are what I would consider "side hustles." As a quick aside, if you ever want to learn about building a side hustle that could take over your full-time income, be sure to look up Nick Loper. I interviewed him on my Year of Purpose Podcast and he has some great books and blogs out there.

A secondary form of income is passive income, also referred to as recurring income. My passive income comes in many forms. For starters, every time someone buys one of my books on Amazon, whether it be in Kindle, paperback, or audiobook format, I receive a monthly royalty check. This is awesome because, each month, I get a deposit directly into my bank account and the hard work is done; the book was already made. The only downside is that if you don't keep up with the marketing of the book, the sales will quickly dwindle. Two years (and counting) later, I still receive monthly checks for my first book, *Life Re-Scripted.* It's not much, but it adds up over time, and remember, these will be around indefinitely.

Third is income that has come from what I consider hobby or side hustles. I've ventured into the world of Fiverr, Upwork (formerly known as Elance), and many other online methods of making money for selling my creative services. In fact, I found a way to bring in $1,000 in one month by simply selling video animations on Fiverr.com, which was a really fun experiment.

I also receive money from cash-back apps that we'll discuss in a later chapter. I've been paid for my public speaking, consulting, selling old items I don't need, and more.

If you think you'll get paid for your passion right away, just know that it might not pay dividends for a very long time.

So don't quit your day job or business. My video business is truly the only thing that allows me to support my lifestyle full time. As I mentioned previously, I've been able to hit the road for any time length that I'd like and still profit. It's possible to run a business virtually and I'm living proof, but that wasn't the first step I took when I set out on that venture.

Passion Isn't Perfect

The reason I say passion isn't perfect is because it's not this magical end-all solution to your problems. It's great if you have something you really care about, but, unless the rest of the world cares about it too, it's very hard to make a profit. Is there at least someone else out there in the world who supports what you do? Absolutely! Is there someone out there in the world who will pay you for what you do? Undoubtedly. However, it takes time and patience to build and grow.

You'll learn many things on the way, but just start out knowing that your passion won't soar like a jet engine right off the bat. You'll need a lot of patience so going in with the mindset that things won't be perfect fresh out of the gate is a fantastic way to set yourself up for growth.

You'll need excitement on your site for your passion to expand so don't get frustrated when the going gets tough.

Be Better

When I first started my video company, I wanted to be the best in my field and remain the go-to videographer for my clients. This was partially because I'm hyper ambitious but also because I need to stand out from the crowd.

It doesn't matter if you're passionate about underwater basket weaving or solving a Rubik's Cube while jumping out of an airplane. If you're going to do it and get paid for it, you're going to have to be better than a lot of other people.

That means taking the time and money to invest in yourself and hone your craft. If it means taking a full year before you can launch your passion business, then do it. Who wants to half-ass anything?

You'll find that you stand out instantly when your service, product, and the way you handle your business go unmatched.

Delegate

When I first started my business, I found that I was doing a lot of things on my own. In fact, I was doing so much that I never had time to get any work completed! This was because I thought that I would save money and it was the smart thing to do. But, one by one, I started to delegate tasks out. For example, taxes, those evil little forms that have to be filled out every year are a royal pain in my behind. When I hired an accountant and paid him $575 to do them for me, I found that not only could I get more money back in my tax return but also I could take the weeks that I'd spend trying to do them right and carry on with my business.

Sure, it seemed like a huge expense to slap that money down on another person and trust them to do it right. But I went with my gut that was telling me I needed to get a professional to do this because it simply wasn't my cup of tea.

I quickly discovered that the $575 I put down could be written off as a business expense and my mind was at ease. But what did I learn from this situation?

It's important to delegate the mind-numbing activities that suck your time up and leave you with nothing, even if it requires payment.

Surround Yourself

This one is plain and simple, surround yourself with other passionate people and stay motivated.

Jim Rohn said, "You are the average of the five people you spend the most time with." If that's the case, then look around at who those people are. Pick out the people who aren't helping you become a better person and ditch them for new, supportive friends!

Find local meetup groups, networking events, and other hobbies that you can immerse yourself in, so that you can discover how other people have taken their passions and coaxed them into profits. Take someone out for coffee after a tai chi class or ask a new friend from a networking group if they go to any other events that you might enjoy.

You'll find more ideas that you can start to dig into in the following chapters, so I won't go into much detail here, but just know that things take time, Rome wasn't built in a day, and you can't do it all on your own.

Chapter 22: How to Make Money Online

Ahh, the holy grail...

Making money online is easy! Simply pay me $1,000 and a monthly fee of just $500 a month for the next twelve months, and I'll teach you to be rich! Just kidding. It's not that simple.

I've played with hundreds of ways to make money on the Internet. Everything from day trading crypto currencies to my college days when I took surveys online and made $30-40 a week lying to survey websites about my experience as an Indian working class fifty-year-old.

Okay, I just made that part up, but I did take surveys and I did make up a lot of answers just to get the cash.

There are literally thousands of ways to make money online, and if you asked me which one works the best, to be honest, I'd have to say all of them and none of them, depending on how much time and effort you put into it.

I want to share with you fifty ways that you can make money in the digital world. I discovered these from many great websites including Lifehacker, Reddit, The Penny Hoarder, Scott Alan Turner, and more. Here are just a *few* ways you can get started:

1. Freelance writing and editing
2. Freelance graphic design
3. Freelance programming
4. Freelance customer service
5. Freelance Internet marketing
6. Freelance translating
7. Freelance transcribing
8. Affiliate marketing
9. Sell crafts, art, or handmade items
10. YouTube adsense
11. Flip pre-built websites filled with content
12. Blog
13. Paid surveys
14. Dropshipping
15. Investing/trading
16. Loaning money
17. Membership website
18. Cashback apps
19. Virtual assistant
20. Ebates (more on this later)
21. Drive for Uber/Lyft
22. Airbnb your home
23. Sell old stuff
24. Open a new credit card from a bonus offer
25. Deliver Amazon packages in your free time
26. Secret shopper
27. Amazon Mechanical Turk

28. Proofread documents
29. Online mock juror
30. Part-time bookkeeping
31. Sell your smartphone photos
32. Teach English
33. Task Rabbit
34. Wear T-shirts (seriously look up Jason Zook - I interviewed him about how he built a million dollar business wearing other company's shirts)
35. Write and sell an ebook
36. Speak and sell audiobooks
37. Create an app
38. Offer gigs on Fiverr, Guru, or Upwork
39. Website tester
40. Online travel agent
41. Online focus groups
42. Flip domain names
43. Sell stock photos/footage
44. Design and sell t-shirts
45. Build a Shopify store
46. Coaching/consulting
47. Micro-investing (look up Acorns App)
48. Use Ibotta for rebates
49. Rent your clothing (or car) with sites like Loanables or Turo
50. Resell concert tickets

There are tons of ways to make money online and those fifty only took about five minutes for me to come up with. Many of them are opportunities I've toyed around with myself!

Ultimately, what it comes down to is you have to start somewhere. You may need to learn a new skill, and, sure, it'll be uncomfortable for a little bit. But this is how businesses are built. People try different things that they've never done before, discover that they have a knack for something, and then spread it out into the world.

But Zephan (you think to yourself), *how in the world will I learn these new skills? I'm already broke!*

Right now, pull out a computer or a phone and go to Fiverr.com because there's literally a man selling a gig titled "I will sing happy birthday in just a thong" for twenty dollars, and he has over one thousand reviews meaning he has made twenty thousand dollars at minimum! This also isn't his only gig, he has four other gigs ranging in price from ten to thirty dollars that have sold at least one thousand more times.

Now I'm not telling you to go ahead and undress and start prostituting yourself virtually for the enjoyment of others. But what I'm trying to say is that, every day, someone out there is becoming a millionaire because they got drunk one night, had a silly idea, and it caught on like wildfire. Capiche?

Chapter 23: Where to Learn New Skills

A year ago, I was prepping for a wedding as one of the groomsmen and had to learn how to fold a pocket square on the spot.

None of the other groomsmen knew how, and they just started stuffing what looked like a handkerchief into the pocket assuming they could blow their noses in it should it be a cold day or they felt like crying. I digress.

So, I was standing in the hotel room with a bunch of gentlemen who were fully capable of putting on their tuxes but had no idea where they would learn to fold a pocket square thirty minutes before the wedding ceremony. I pulled out my phone, opened up YouTube, and simply typed, "how to fold a pocket square" and the first video to come up was titled, "How to Fold a Pocket Square: Five Easy Ways to Fold a Pocket Square."

It can't get much simpler than that. You can learn nearly anything on YouTube. It doesn't matter if you're trying to learn about reducing sciatic nerve pain or you just want to know how long to bake a turkey in the oven (yes I've looked up both of these things). YouTube is a wonderful resource that has years' worth of content uploaded every single day. As of 2017, nearly five billion videos are watched on YouTube per day and three hundred hours of videos are uploaded every minute. There's something for everyone.

It still boggles my mind every time someone asks me a question about something I clearly don't know, yet they won't take thirty seconds to search it and find the answer. When I worked at the Apple Store, we were taught to respond, "I don't know, but let's find out *together,*" which was one of the best things I ever learned. Let's find out together. It's simple, yet it inspires us to take action and empowers us with knowledge.

If you're feeling like it might be impossible to learn a new skill (which I know is false) just watch my friend Stephen Robinson's TEDx Talk on YouTube called The Curious Person's Guide To Learning Anything. He also has over one hundred videos on his popular YouTube channel (http://www.zephanmoses.com/52skillz) appropriately titled 52Skillz where he learned one new skill a week for a year.

Stephen said, "Learning is easy, motivating yourself to learn is the hard part." He goes on to talk about other forces like school, work, and family preventing him from moving forward and learning a new skill.

Which brings me back to the beginning; why did you pick up this book in the first place? Perhaps you just wanted to go to Europe for the first time in your life. Maybe you were thinking if you made some extra cash and took a nice vacation, it would reinvigorate your life. Whatever the reason may be, you're going to encounter forces like this throughout your life, but if you want to learn a new skill, you have to push back and balance out everything going on. This creates space in your life for growth.

Assuming that YouTube isn't this almighty encyclopedic resource that I think it is, where else can you learn a new skill?

Here are 50 websites you can use to learn a new skill:

CreativeLive	DuoLingo
OfficeHours	Investopedia
Coach.me	Bigger Pockets
edX	Mixergy
General Assembly	Memrise
Treehouse	Rype
Skillcrush	iTunesU
Highbrow	One Month
Lynda	Calm
Coursmos	Bodybuilding
CodeAcademy	Livestrong
SkillShare	Nomadicmatt
Ted Talks	Lonely Planet
Udacity	Wandering Trader
Coursera	52Skillz
MIT's Open CourseWare	Curious
99u	Free Code Camp
Udemy	Platzi
SkilledUp	Code School
OpenSesame	Code.org
Babbel	Dash
Savvy.is	DataMonkey
Thinkful	Lingvist
SitePoint	Guide.co
Khan Academy	Pianu

As you can see, there are many ways that you can go about picking up a new skill. Coding has been a very popular one over the recent years because it's a highly desired trade. But whether it's learning a new instrument (Pianu) or learning to meditate (Calm) there are plenty of ways you can do so absolutely free of charge

Chapter 24: How to Make Your Money Work for You

One of my best mentors taught me that getting rich isn't about making a lot of money. It's about learning how to make your money work for you, and they were right.

I've watched one of my investment portfolios increase steadily at 20% per year, and all I do is add $150 a month. The account is about to pass $15,000, and I've only been using it for a little over a year. In case you're doing the math on that, I started out with a good sum of money, but it's also making me a good sum of money.

Neil Patel's, in *I Will Teach You to Be Rich,* talks about how most Americans don't even have an emergency fund of $500, but those who do are keeping it, more often than not, in one of the big banks such as Wells Fargo, Bank of America, etc. Even if you have $10,000 sitting in a savings account, you might only be getting an interest rate of 0.01% when you could be getting a rate as high as 1.30% with an online bank. The only difference is convenience and ease of use.

Let's do some math on this just to show you an example of how $10,000 would grow over time if you used each bank:

Time	Big Bank (0.01% APY)	Online Bank (1.30% APY)
After five years	$10,005	$10,667
After ten years	$10,010	$11,378
After fifteen years	$10,015	$12,137
After twenty years	$10,020	$12,947

And this is just assuming that your money is compounding yearly, but it shows the difference the money makes. This also doesn't take into account the fact that you'd, hopefully, be adding additional cash into the account over those five, ten, or even twenty years. In the end, I'll take the additional $2,947 for doing zero work any day.

If you're interested in online banking, look into banks like Ally, Synchrony, Barclays, and American Express.

Now that I've proven to you what your money will do for you when you put it in the right place, let's discuss a few options for leveraging your cash.

Vanguard Funds

Vanguard Funds, also known as an ETF (Exchange Traded Fund), are built like a mutual fund but priced and traded on the stock market like an individual stock. They combine the advantages of mutual funds with the trading flexibility of continual pricing of individual securities.

What this mean in plain English is that somewhere in a building, there's a guy on a computer who uses really smart math to determine what stocks to buy from what companies and he buys a lot of it. We're talking billions of dollars moving around each day. But instead of you having to make the decisions of whom to buy stock from, he takes a small fee called a commission and you can buy stock in his collection of stocks.

Why is this a good idea?

Well, for starters, you don't have to educate yourself about hundreds of companies, read up about how they did with their quarterly earnings reports, research future estimates, or any of that nonsense.

Typically, these would be considered very safe bets because companies like Vanguard are very good at what they do. On top of all of this, some Vanguard funds are set up to behave based on what year you'd like to retire.

If you'd like to check one of them out, go ahead and Google "Vanguard Target Retirement 2050 Fund Investor Shares." It trades as VFIFX and is a solid bet for someone planning to retire in the year 2050. It's a more aggressive fund and then slowly eases its way into more secure stocks and bonds as it nears the year 2050.

I won't go into all the details here, and I'm in no way recommending you should buy this ETF. But this is a great example of a "stock" that has returned nearly 20% year to date.

Betterment

Betterment is my secret go-to tool that I keep in my back pocket and recommend to anyone and everyone. I mentioned it earlier because I've received a 20% return on my money and I only add $150 a month every month. It's a small chunk of change that grows bigger and bigger by the day.

Betterment is a simple app and website that allows you to see the long game when it comes to investing. Not only do they allow their users to gain 2.66% more per year than a typical investor but they also use special tools to lower taxes and fees and diversify your portfolio, which allows you to be a smarter investor.

Think of Betterment as a robo-advisor or a really smart online stock picker that does all the heavy lifting for you. They purchase ETFs like the Vanguard fund mentioned prior and allow you to make money by only having to buy a percentage of a share. Meaning if the fund is $100 a share but you only have $50, you can still buy 50% of a stock and let your money grow.

They also have great tools for predicting where your money could be in forty, fifty, or even sixty years, and it automates it. You literally don't even have to touch it once it's set up, and you could find yourself with a cool million dollar retirement fund down the line if you play your cards right.

Betterment is the epitome of having your money work for you.

401K, IRA, Roth IRA and More

Whenever someone tells me their job offers them a 401K, IRA, Roth IRA, or anything else, I recommend they take it. When I worked for Apple, there was a stock purchase program that allowed me to buy stock at 25% off the price from the previous quarter, which is insane because they're on their way to becoming the first trillion dollar company.

When employers provide a 401K, there's usually some form of matching, which should be read as "free money." While I'm not a financial advisor, I must say if you do have the opportunity to open any or all of these accounts, it's usually a good idea.

The quicker your money can start working for you, the better, and if your employer is going to double what you put into your 401K, you might as well take the free cash.

Micro Loans

I first discovered the idea of a micro loan from a website called Kiva. Kiva allows you to loan out money for entrepreneurs doing amazing things all over the world, and then, over time, they pay you back with interest. It's a really simple way to throw a few hundred or thousand dollars somewhere that has a high rate of paying back all of the money loaned.

I've also discovered on Reddit, specifically in the r/borrow subreddit, located at https://www.reddit.com/r/borrow/, there's a group of people who need assistance and simply state how much they need, how much money they'll pay back (including interest), and when it will be paid back. Most users loan through PayPal to keep things safe and secure, but it's another easy way to make some cash when you have extra money sitting around.

****

These are just a few ways to make sure that your money works for you. In the end, the best way to do this is to speak with a financial advisor and get professional advice on where to place your money. If you receive an inheritance or gifts from time to time, I recommend investing, not spending.

Chapter 25: How to Get Paid to Travel

There are tons of ways you can get paid to travel. My favorite was working with my local youth group because, every summer, they send hundreds of teens on summer trips throughout the world. I was fortunate enough to get picked to lead a trip to Italy, Slovenia, Vatican City, England, France, Holland, and Belgium. They paid for all of my expenses including meals, hotels, transportation, and airfare. On top of all of this, they paid me a stipend of $1,000 for the five-week trip.

So for starters, there are many organizations and nonprofits that need trip leaders, even if you have no prior experience. For the trip that I went on, I had experience traveling, which was a huge plus, but we had a tour guide with us throughout the entire trip, so I never had to tell our teens the history and significance of the Rosetta Stone or talk about Pompeii. I highly recommend this if you have a local youth group, church group, or anything else; that will be your best place to start.

There are plenty of other opportunities to travel and get paid while you do it. Let's start with WWOOFing.

WWOOF

WWOOF, also known as Worldwide Opportunities on Organic Farms is a great chance for volunteers to choose a set time when they work on a farm with travelers in exchange for a place to live and meals. This is a bit different than getting paid with cash, since you're getting paid with a place to stay and food.

There are flexible terms, so you can WWOOF as long or as short as you'd like. You'll have to cover your airfare to get there, but once you arrive, you'll have pretty much everything you need.

Teach English

I have multiple college friends who've gone over to Asia and taught English there. It's very common in Asia, the Middle East, and Latin America for English-speaking natives with a bachelor's degree to teach "the direct method" in which students learn through being immersed in the language.

You'll be a highly desired candidate if you have a TEFL (Teaching English as a Foreign Language) certification and make between $35-45K/year doing it.

Seasonal

I have an acquaintance who started as a seasonal employee for a ski resort, and when he started making videos for them, they ultimately hired him full time to run their video and social media department. But even if you aren't tech savvy but know how to ski, there are tons of resorts around the U.S. (California, Colorado, etc.) or even abroad (New Zealand) that are looking for employees.

It's a great chance to get away from the city life, but if you're like me and your body wasn't made for the cold, perhaps check out working on a cruise ship or perhaps going down to the Caribbean seasonally!

Au Pair

Just as I wasn't built for the cold, you may not be the best candidate for this. But if you're someone who loves working with young children, there are families all over the world seeking an Au Pair to take care of their kids. You get free room and board along with payment, so it's not a bad gig!

Check out www.aupairworld.com for more details.

Birthright

Birthright programs aren't just for Jews, although if you do have a Jewish heritage, leading a trip to Israel is a good opportunity. You should check out programs geared toward other cultures such as Birthright Armenia, Heritage

Greece, ReConnect Hungary, and the Love Boat Study Program.

Adventure

When I say adventure, I don't mean go outside and start walking. I mean you could be a team member working on the Canary Islands or in Montenegro, receiving food and accommodations along with competitive pay and travel expenses in exchange for running group activities like rafting, archery, ropes courses, and more. They usually only require you to be 18 or over and have some experience working with children or adults. Look at www.adventurework.co.uk for more.

House Sitting

Head on over to www.trustedhousesitters.com where you'll find people all over the world who want their pets and houses taken care of. You register as a member for just over $100 and then you become a verified house and pet sitter. In this particular opportunity, your payment is being able to cuddle up with a furry one and have a gorgeous house to yourself, but this can save you a ton of money while on the road.

Flight Attendant

This one is a bit more obvious but if you don't mind having a constantly changing schedule and making around $50K per year, becoming a flight attendant can be a great way to see the world for free. You'll land in a different destination every day that you work, and the average attendant only works about 80 hours a month. So, this means you'll have lots of time to see the world.

Cruise Lines

Working on a cruise ship can send you to exotic locations but it comes with long hours, low pay, and cramped living quarters. But if you're looking for something a bit more enticing, check out becoming a steward/stewardess or deckhand on a luxury yacht. They've even created a TV show out of it called *Below Deck on Bravo*. The pay is much better, but the work is even tougher. If you're up for the challenge, go for it!

Travel Blogger

When I was conducting my Year of Purpose Podcast, I interviewed a couple who created a page called *How Far From Home*. You can learn more about Stevo and Chanel at http://howfarfromhome.com/ where they document their journey from working in the advertising and branding industry to ultimately quitting their jobs and traveling the world. They now get paid to deliver talks, partner with organizations on videos, and overall live their best life.

****

So, you see, there are abundant opportunities for traveling the world and getting paid to do it. Now let's move into some of my favorite apps that I use to get paid without doing a whole lot of work.

Chapter 26: Apps That Pay You

Do you remember as a kid when your parents sat down at the kitchen table with a pair of scissors and a stack of coupons? In my house, we'd sit down and go through every single coupon that came in the mail and determine if we'd eat it. If we would, we'd cut it out and sort it into categories like toiletries, poultry, produce, etc.

As technology improved over time, many places realized that cutting coupons was annoying and wasteful, so they started to offer rebates. These rebates started to transform into cash back offers that would automatically be sent to your bank account via PayPal. This is exactly what I leverage any time I buy something online.

Ebates

I'll be the first to say that I absolutely love Ebates. It's a small extension that gets installed on Google Chrome or on your mobile device. On the computer, it tracks what stores you visit, and whenever you land on a website that participates with Ebates, it pops up in the corner with a notification showing you how much cash back you can receive on your purchase. The best part is they partner with thousands of stores that you already shop from. What's more, you can refer friends, and you'll get $25 when they sign up, and your friend will receive $10.

You can try it out for yourself right now by going to: http://www.zephanmoses.com/ebates

If you use this link, I get some cash, but you also get cash! Be sure to invite your friends because you can get bonuses just for inviting them. You don't even have to buy anything! Each month, you'll get what they call a "big fat check" sent directly to your PayPal email address and then you can cash out to your bank account for free.

Smile

Have you ever heard of Smile? Of course you have! But not in the sense of a facial expression. Smile is a division of Amazon where you can choose a charity and any time you make a purchase on smile.amazon.com, a percentage of the proceeds go to your charity of choice.

Amazon Smile doesn't pay out directly to your bank account but it can pay dividends to a great cause that you want to support without you having to do any more work. Being able to donate to a charity pays back in more ways than one.

RetailMeNot

Another website that I'm constantly spending time at is www.retailmenot.com. Again, this one doesn't pay me directly, but it provides promotional codes that can be applied on many websites across the Internet that you're already shopping. This, in turn, allows you to save money and ultimately put cash back into your pocket.

Here's a list of a few more apps that you can download directly to your phone and start making cash with:

- Rover - A dog-walking app that connects you with people in your area. I've tested this out myself and made upwards of $35 per walk per day!
- Gigwalk - Connecting users to businesses looking to get local contract work done, including taking photos of store displays, testing mobile apps, delivery services, mystery shopping, and more.
- Surveys On The Go - Fortune 500 companies, major political campaigns, and jury trials you see in the headlines every day need user opinions and this app will pay users for participating in them.
- Ibotta - Shop for your regular products and brands to earn cash. This one is very similar to Ebates!
- Airbnb - Do you have a home? Do you have an extra room in your home? Now you can rent it out and make money by having people stay with you instead of in a hotel.
- Uber/Lyft - If you have a car in great shape and it isn't a decade old, you can drive in your spare time and make some extra cash.
- Shopkick - How would you like incentives to check out specific stores and items in those stores? You can earn more by making purchases that Shopkick recommends.

- Checkpoints - Watch videos and scan barcodes to earn points; then you can redeem them for gift cards on sites like Amazon.
- App Trailers - Watch videos of apps in the app store and get rewarded via PayPal for it!
- IconZoomer - Complete assignments by taking photos and uploading them. Share your thoughts on market products while you're at it for more PayPal cash.
- GymPact - Users have to make a weeklong pact on GymPact to work out, get paid for every day you go and pay a penalty for every workout that you miss.

There are plenty of apps out there just waiting to pay you. As usual, you won't become a millionaire or even a thousandaire from using them, but if you have free time and you want to be more productive, these are just a few ideas to get you going.

Another thing to mention is that Uber and Lyft have incentive programs where you can cash in on inviting your friends. It's very similar to Ebates in that they want to gain users and they know they'll make more money if you add five, ten, or fifteen of your friends, so they pay out big bucks.

It's also worth saying that apps come and go, opportunities do get leveraged, and, from time to time, they can be shut down. I wish it were possible to keep this book up to date, but some of these apps may not work by the time you discover them, or offers may be gone. It's simply the nature of the beast. But if I've introduce you to at least one new way that you can get paid, then I've done my job!

Chapter 27: Affiliate Marketing & Blogging

Affiliate marketing has been around for a really long time. You may have noticed in the previous chapter, I showed you a link for Ebates where you can sign up and get some free cash. However, when you sign up, I get some cash too. This is essentially what an affiliate link is, a special link that a website uses to track who clicked it and who's responsible for referring the sale. It's awesome because it's really simple, and it's one of the easiest ways to make money online, dating back to when people first started making money through blogging and social media.

There's a great affiliate program available for Amazon called Amazon Associates. I've used it over the years any time I wrote a blog post and referred to an Amazon product that I loved. And when someone made a purchase from my link, I got a commission. I have to give a warning here because some people are tempted to just go out and link to anything and everything in hopes that people will click and they'll make money.

The reality is that people have caught on to this, so it's really important to A) only link to things you've bought yourself and endorse and B) provide a transparent warning that when someone uses that link you'll be getting a kickback. This is ethical, and, in some cases, it may be required by law. So, in case you haven't noticed in my previous chapters, some links in this book are affiliate links, and, yes, they can give me a kickback. I try to be as open as possible, though, because I only want to use affiliate programs that you can benefit from. Think of it like sending me a small tip for my recommendation that requires little work on your end.

If you're just getting your feet wet, I'd look at the Amazon program because it's widely used. If you have a blog, you can start to write about different products you've used. Perhaps you write about cooking and you had to buy a food scale that you really liked. You could then link to the food scale, and, any time someone buys it, you'll get around 4%, which is nothing if only one person buys, but if you have a big enough following and 100 people buy it, you'll get a nice check each month.

Here are some pros for affiliate marketing:

- It's free to get started; you simply sign up for the program. There's no price of admission.
- You don't actually have to create a product or service. You can make money by selling other people's products. (Be careful with this.)
- You don't have to manufacture or have inventory.
- You can work whenever you want.
- This can be incorporated into an existing blog.

Here are some of the downsides:

- It can take a really long time to get enough people clicking your links, and building up an audience isn't always easy.
- A bad product can ruin your reputation, so be careful who you endorse.
- You don't have any control over the product, quality, or really anything once someone clicks the link.
- Some companies never pay out, even though they claim they will. But this can also happen if you don't set things up properly.
- Competition – everyone is doing it so it's tough to compete.

So, there are, of course, two edges to this sword. I've made a few thousand dollars as an affiliate with Amazon and a few courses and programs that I've taken and endorsed. It's possible and just takes time. Research thoroughly before diving right in.

Blogging can incorporate affiliate links but there are ways to make money as a blogger that don't involve links. As a blogger, if you write really good content and you sell different services like coaching or conferences, you can make a ton of money from your audience.

Another thing you can do is create your own products and blog around them. Let's come up with a hypothetical…

Let's say you identify a problem in your life and you've found a way to fix it. For example, I wear glasses and they get smudged all the time. I could 1) bring a microfiber cloth with me everywhere 2) pay extra for stronger lenses that don't scratch as easily although this isn't a total fix or 3) develop a product like a spray of some sort that coats my glasses, only needs to be applied every month, and prevents all smudges. Now I'm not saying this doesn't already exist, nor do I have any clue how to do this, but if I have this magical product, I'm going to want to generate sales.

I could start by going to social media and building Facebook and Instagram marketing tactics. But I could also just start blogging about it.

Think about it. What if I wrote thirty articles about taking care of your glasses?

Now I know what you're thinking, *How on earth will he come up with thirty topics about glasses?* It's funny you should ask because when I type into Google, "how to clean glasses," Google recommends the following:

- How to clean glasses
- How to clean glasses cloth
- How to clean glasses nose pads
- How to clean glasses with spray
- How to clean glasses wipes
- How to clean glasses transition lenses

The list goes on and on, and as soon as I change the wording of my Google search, the search engine will recommend even more topics for me, based on what people are already looking for!

How cool is that?

Google can tell you exactly what to write about, especially when it's a ridiculous topic such as cleaning glasses. Now I've built an entire blog around glasses, and I've laid the foundation for an audience of people searching for these terms to find my crazy awesome product.

This is just one possibility. You could also leverage Amazon affiliate links in your blog posts to microfiber cloths, glasses cases, and more!

If you're ready to test the waters with blogging, I recommend making a free website through SquareSpace. It's a great place to start without having to learn how to program a website.

Happy blogging!

Chapter 28: Writing a Book

TL:DR (Too Long, Didn't Read) – No, self-publishing didn't make me rich, and chances are that it won't make you rich either. But that's not why I did it, and here's how it can change your life.

When I first set off into the Year of Purpose Podcast and the world of online businesses, I never had the intention of monetizing it, and, still, to this day, it isn't the reason why I'm able to put food on my table.

As most of you know, I have a video production company, which is 99.9% of my income.

But I wanted to share an open and honest look into my side hustle income as of February 9th, 2017, meaning I was just one year and one month from having launched my first book, *Life Re-Scripted.*

Now don't get me wrong, I loved the entire process of writing that book and I've learned so many things along the way that will allow me to make my next book even bigger and better. In fact, starting that book was a big reason why I'm writing this book (my fifth one)!

So let's begin with a transparent look into how much my book paid me...

I did a book launch party when we first launched on Amazon. I originally was planning to have twenty of my closest friends and relatives but it quickly grew.
It grew so much that we had fifty-six people buy tickets in advance of my event for a total of $1,028.79.

For that event, I bought a box of a hundred copies of my book from Createspace.com (Amazon's self-publishing wing that prints my books on demand) for a total of $351.46 and I bought sixty T-shirts for the event at $6 each for a total of $360.

When you subtract the cost of the books and the T-shirts, you're left with $317.33 in profit.

I also bought a couple bottles of wine and a small cheese plate for the event and paid a photographer to shoot photos. I may have walked away with $200 in my pocket for the launch event when all was said and done.

Once the book launched on Amazon, there were three different places you could buy: paperback via Amazon CreateSpace, Kindle via the Amazon KDP store, and audiobook via ACX.

One year into my book being available for sales, here are the totals:

CreateSpace Paperback: $308.35
*This doesn't include the hundred books I bought for the launch party

Kindle: $391.20

Audiobook: $101.85

This leaves my total profit one year later (including book launch party profits) at approximately $1,001.40
To be really honest about where the profit is, it's only fair that I include a few other things I spent money on.

Here are my expenses for getting the book made:

Book Cover Design: $316.07 (I wouldn't change a thing)

Book Formatting (Print/Kindle): $150

This was from a freelancer on Upwork.com whom I had a hard time getting hold of three-quarters of the way through. She did a great job, but communication was poor toward the end. Be sure to give yourself time and hire someone who does the formatting manually. Some people try to pass your content through an automated software that doesn't work properly and say that they did it manually. The only way to know for sure is to hire someone who does the full layout in Adobe InDesign or Adobe Illustrator.

Book Editor/Proofreader: $150

Again, this was a freelancer from Upwork.com with whom I had a mediocre experience. Still, to this day, some words are misspelled that she should have caught. Be sure to hire a native English-speaking editor and check out their rating and reviews. I would say plan on budgeting closer to $500 to hire the best to properly format and edit your book.

Self-Publishing School Course: $597

This was a fantastic investment. I have to give Chandler Bolt some serious credit here, as this course was worth every penny and more. I couldn't have done it without his course. If you want to start with the free How to Self Publish Course, you can visit http://www.zephanmoses.com/sps.

So how much did I spend on getting the book into existence? $1,213.07. And how much did I make from the book? $1,001.40, which leaves me at a deficit of -$211.67

Some might see that as a complete failure.

I see it as a complete success, and here's why...
I couldn't tell you how many interactions I've had over the last twelve months when I've been able to use my book as a platform and a networking conversation starter.

I couldn't tell you how many times I've been invited to speak in front of a crowd whether it was three people or three hundred people.

I couldn't tell you how many people all over the world have written to me, telling me how they changed their lives because they read my book.

And lastly, I couldn't tell you how many people's lives will be impacted because someone who was inspired by my story made a change in their life that benefitted others.

But I know that it happened.

I know that there are high schoolers out there who are getting ready to go to college and might change their major because of it. I know that some of them might decide it's okay to take the path less traveled and become an entrepreneur. I know that someone out there might become a doctor and cure a disease that has been incurable up until now. I know that there are members of my fraternity who heard me speak and have been inspired to interview hundreds of people just as I have so that they too can determine their path to success. I know that I have siblings who look up to me now more than ever.

I know that I made a difference.

So why self publish a book if you're just going to lose money?

My question to you is why not?

If you have a message or a story and there's an audience out there willing to learn a lesson or two, then write it down. You won't be around forever, and you can only directly interact with a limited number of people in your lifetime. So, leave a written and recorded legacy of your life experiences and wisdom that will benefit many more people in years to come.

Don't wait.

Plus, for all we know, your book could be a lot more successful than my first book. There was a lot of marketing and planning that went into it and it certainly has paid off in other aspects of my life. There's also a very good reason why I'm now on my fifth book; over time, it does pay off, and I do get a check every single month from Amazon.

So, don't go into self-publishing thinking you'll become rich, but also don't knock it until you've tried it!

My Message to You

Dear reader,

I hope that, in some way, shape, or form, this book has encouraged you to take a leap of faith. Whether that leap is to get on an airplane for the first time, to fix your credit/debt situation, or to simply start making some extra cash online.

When my entrepreneurial journey began, I was simply a guy with a college degree and a few useful skills. I don't think of myself as someone who has any special abilities or as someone who lived my life differently than anyone else.

Every possibility that you discover in life was once an impossibility. From landing on the moon to running a four-minute mile (first completed in 1954), the sky is truly the limit both literally and figuratively.

Travel hacking has changed my life. It has improved my credit score beyond belief and allows me to take a weekend out to go see friends on the other side of the country whenever I feel like it. The world works differently now than it did a few decades ago. We found a better way to leverage the world to our advantage.

We created and built new tools, systems, and ideas that changed the very fabric of our society.

I believe in us.

I believe in our innate ability to do things differently.

I believe we'll be the ones to change the world.

But first, it starts with ourselves.

Take a good look inside, deep down, and think about what you'd like out of life. Focus on that, harness the positive energy that courses through your veins, and don't stop until you get every last ounce and drop that life has to offer.

Henry Ford said, "When everything seems to be going against you, remember that the airplane takes off against the wind, not with it."

Thank you for being a small part of my journey by purchasing this book. If you found the skills in here useful, please leave a review and mention your favorite part of the book on Amazon. I read every single one of them. Now go out there and hack your way across the planet!

www.ingramcontent.com/pod-product-compliance
Lightning Source LLC
Chambersburg PA
CBHW031319040426
42443CB00005B/134